"Book by book across the whole biblical canvas, Linebaugh shows how Scripture doesn't just talk about good news for sufferers and sinners, but bursts from the page, bringing real comfort to real people from the living God."

—Simeon Zahl
University of Cambridge

"I have been teaching the Bible for church groups and in seminary classes for a long time now, and from the beginning I have been on the hunt for an accessible guide that surveys the Bible's contents *and* shows how it all fits together theologically around the good news about Jesus. . . . My search is now over: this is that book."

—Wesley Hill
Western Theological Seminary

"I will return to this book time and again as I consider—and encourage others to ponder—how best to approach and appropriate Holy Scripture."

—Todd D. Still
Truett Theological Seminary

"A stunning reminder that the Scriptures do not just teach—they reveal and heal. With theological clarity and pastoral warmth, Linebaugh shows how the Word of God exposes our need and meets it with the grace of Christ."

—Justin S. Holcomb
bishop of the Episcopal Diocese of Central Florida

"In this learned, artful, and deeply pastoral book, Linebaugh helps his readers realize that it is the work of God through his Word to change us, not our work to change ourselves by the Word for God."

—Ashley Null
bishop of the Anglican Diocese of North Africa

"This book provides an introduction to the Bible that is both crystal clear and theologically profound. Linebaugh offers fresh insights throughout and demonstrates brilliantly how the Scriptures provide two precious and sorely needed gifts: honesty about ourselves and hope for the future in God."

—John M. G. Barclay
Durham University

"Here is pastoral theology at its best, linking the diagnostic and liberating power of [the] living Word with the hurts and hopes of human hearts. Take up and read!"

—**Susan Eastman**
Duke Divinity School

"God was in Christ, and Linebaugh capably shows us how Christ speaks life now through these words of his prophets and apostles. For instruction, for comfort, for resurrection, Linebaugh shows us how Christ graces us again and again through these life-giving words."

—**Michael Allen**
Reformed Theological Seminary

"A highly enjoyable read that packs a truly impressive amount of information and insight on the whole of the Bible into such a short space. It deserves a very wide readership."

—**Simon Gathercole**
University of Cambridge

"In this slender volume, Linebaugh invites us into a relationship with Scripture, illuminating throughout the relentlessness of human wrong as it encounters the greater relentlessness of God's grace."

—**Beverly Roberts Gaventa**
Princeton Theological Seminary

"The word 'invitation' in the subtitle of this book is a key one: Linebaugh is a delightfully charming, welcoming guide. . . . Like George Herbert, the presiding saint here, Linebaugh shares with us holy wonderment at the Book in which, amazingly, 'heaven lies flat.'"

—**Alan Jacobs**
Baylor University

"Linebaugh's invitation to Scripture is just that—not an invitation to itself so that readers marvel at its cleverness, but an invitation to something beyond itself, an invitation to join the author in his love for God's word. . . . Readers will be drawn into the love of God communicated through the piercing honesty of the biblical text."

—**Amy Peeler**
Wheaton College

The Well That Washes What It Shows

An Invitation to Holy Scripture

Jonathan A. Linebaugh

William B. Eerdmans Publishing Company
Grand Rapids, Michigan

Wm. B. Eerdmans Publishing Co.
2006 44th Street SE, Grand Rapids, MI 49508
www.eerdmans.com

Published 2025
Printed in the United States of America

31 30 29 28 27 26 25   1 2 3 4 5 6 7

ISBN 978-0-8028-8548-7

Library of Congress Cataloging-in-Publication Data

A catalog record for this book is available from the Library of Congress.

Biblical quotations are from the English Standard Version unless otherwise noted; quotations designated "AT" are translations by the author.

For those students

&

for Josh—

philologists all

Blessed Lord, who hast caused all holy Scriptures to be written for our learning: Grant that we may in such wise hear them, read, mark, learn, and inwardly digest them, that by patience and comfort of thy holy Word, we may embrace and ever hold fast the blessed hope of everlasting life, which thou hast given us in our Saviour Jesus Christ. Amen.

—Collect for Holy Scripture from
the Book of Common Prayer

Whenever our heart condemns us, God is greater than our heart.

—1 John 3:20

Oh Book! infinite sweetnesse! let my heart
    Suck ev'ry letter, and a hony gain,
    Precious for any grief in any part;
To cleare the breast, to mollifie all pain.

Thou art all health, health thriving till it make
    A full eternitie: thou art a masse
    Of strange delights, where we may wish & take.
Ladies, look here; this is the thankfull glasse,

That mends the lookers eyes: this is the well
    That washes what it shows. Who can indeare
    Thy praise too much? thou art heav'ns Lidger here,
Working against the states of death and hell.

    Thou art joyes handsell: heav'n lies flat in thee,
    Subject to ev'ry mounters bended knee.

—"TheHoly Scriptures I,"
by George Herbert, 1633

Contents

INTRODUCTION

The Story and Shape of Holy Scripture

IN 1633 A PASTOR WROTE A POEM about the Bible. Holy Scripture, celebrated George Herbert, is "infinite sweetness," "precious for any grief," a source of "health" and "joy" and a message of divine mercy and love stronger than "death." Then comes this line: God's word is "the well / That washes what it shows" ("Holy Scripture I," from *The Temple*). "The word of God," as Hebrews 4:12 says, "is living and active." God "spoke," sings Psalm 33:9, "and it came to be." Herbert's poem captures this living and creative power of Holy Scripture with the verbs "washes" and "shows." Holy Scripture is "the well" of God's word, and this "living and active" word does a double work: it "washes" and it "shows." God speaks to show, to unveil honest human need: there is sorrow, bondage, shame, sin, and fear. But God also and finally speaks to wash, to deliver and redeem those in need: there is hope, freedom, mercy, forgiveness, and peace.

About a hundred years before Herbert's poem, a professor named Martin Luther proposed a set of theses in 1518 entitled *For an Inquiry into Truth and for the Consolation of Troubled Consciences.* The two parts of that title capture the two hopes of this book: to hear the truth of Holy Scripture as the word of honesty and hope, God's address that says, "I see and know you" and also "I forgive and forever love you." God's word is a well that shows, surfacing and honestly seeing the weariness, pain, confusion, and fear of life. But this well also washes, speaking what Thomas Cranmer calls the "comfortable words" of God's love in Jesus that give hope to the hurting, ashamed, worn-out, and afraid (Book of Common Prayer).

This book is an introduction to Holy Scripture that hopes to be an invitation to Holy Scripture: to hear and receive what the apostle Paul calls "the gospel of the glory of Christ" (2 Cor. 4:4). This is the "treasure" that "God's word" announces and gives (2 Cor. 4:2, 7). "What we proclaim is not ourselves, but Jesus Christ as Lord" (2 Cor. 4:5). This, according to Paul, is the "ministry" we have "by the mercy of God" (2 Cor. 4:1), the "Father of our Lord Jesus Christ," who is "the Father of mercies and God of all comfort" (2 Cor. 1:3). As Paul asks in another letter to the church in Corinth, "What do you have that you did not receive?" (1 Cor. 4:7). The "treasure" of "the gospel of the glory of Christ" is given as God speaks, and it is held by those who hear "in jars of clay" because "the surpassing power belongs to God and not to us" (2 Cor. 4:7).

Ministry is hearing before it is speaking, receiving before it is giving. Ministering the word entails patiently and prayerfully listening to and receiving the gospel so that the words of pastoral care and proclamation do not morph into "a different gospel" (Gal. 1:6) but remain and are given as the actual and only "gospel of Christ" (Gal. 1:7). Oswald Bayer captures this pattern of ministry: ministers "pass on to others the word they have received." This means, first, that ministers "need to receive the word themselves" and only then announce "that word" in a way that, in the power of Holy Spirit, "it speaks to the hearts of their listeners as God's word for them today." This "one gospel," Bayer concludes, "is an unconditional promise and categorical gift" that gives Jesus Christ, and "it must always be spoken anew without ever saying anything new . . . for the only thing we can say new is what will never again become old": the gospel of Jesus Christ, who said, "Fear not, I am . . . the living one. I died, and behold I am alive forevermore" (Rev. 1:17–18; "Preaching the Word").

—

The book contains three chapters on the Old Testament; three on the New Testament; a chapter on Romans that serves as an interpretative case study, theological synthesis, and pastoral bridge; and then one chapter on how to read the Bible with and as ministry to others. The sequence runs from Genesis to Revelation, through the Bible, encountering the God who, in mercy and grace, came to and called the "weary and heavy-laden" in Jesus (Matt. 11:28, AT). The final section considers what it means to read Holy Scripture and asks how God's powerful and redeeming word might be ministered. This book moves from the source—the Scriptures, where we encounter the gospel and God's word, especially in Jesus Christ—all the way to the horizon of ministry: reading Holy Scripture with and ministering God's word to the "captive" and "sinners" Jesus came to "set free" and "call" (Luke 4:18; 5:32). The God who speaks to us in Holy Scripture is the God who speaks in his Son (Heb. 1:1–2), the God who sent his Son to make us his beloved sons and daughters (Gal. 4:4–7). Because of this gracious speaking and sending, we are invited to speak to God: "our Father," "Abba! Father!" (Matt. 6:9; Gal. 4:7; Rom. 8:15). In and through Holy Scripture, as God the Father, in the power of the Holy Spirit, speaks to us in the Son, we also and forever hear God, by grace, saying to us what he has always said to his eternal Son: "You are my beloved child, in you I am well pleased" (Mark 1:11, AT; 9:7; Luke 3:22).

—

Four questions: What (or who) is the source, the story, the subject, and the shape of Holy Scripture? The texts that are contained in and together constitute the Bible were written by many people, in different times and places, in different styles and genres. For all this variety (and for all the historical questions it entails), those who receive and read this book as Holy Scripture often conclude a reading of any portion or passage with the phrase, "the word of the Lord." This echoes the self-testimony of Scripture. "All Scripture is breathed out by God" (2 Tim. 3:16). As Hebrews says, "Long ago, at many times and in many ways, *God spoke* to our fathers by the prophets" (Heb. 1:1). That the Creator speaks "by the prophets" is an indication of God's grace: God communicates with human creatures in a creaturely way, accommodating the divine address to created and fallen nature by speaking in and through the creaturely word that is the writing of prophets and apostles. As one eighteenth-century author put it, God's word is an "address" from the Creator "to the creature through the creature"—a merciful pattern of divine communication and communion embodied in "the Word became flesh" of the incarnation (John 1:14) and also reflected in the promising words of water, bread, and wine that are baptism and the Lord's Supper (Hamann, *Aesthetica in nuce*).

"By the prophets," however, it is God who speaks. In Hebrews 1:1, God is the subject of the verb: "God spoke." God is the source of Holy Scripture. And because this is the word of the living God, the God who creates and gives life through his let-there-be-word, this "word of the Lord is," as Hebrews also says, "living and active" (Heb. 4:12). As God says through the prophet Isaiah,

> So shall my word be that goes out from my mouth;
> it shall not return to me empty,
> but it shall accomplish that which I purpose,
> and shall succeed in the thing for which I sent it.
> (Isa. 55:11)

This is the living and active word of the Creator who said, "Let there be," and it was (Gen. 1). God's word is also God's work: "For he spoke, and it came to be" (Ps. 33:9).

What God does by speaking—diagnose and deliver, reveal human need and give Christological hope—is the question of the shape of Scripture. But first: story and subject.

One natural way to summarize Scripture is to trace a narrative arc. From Genesis to Revelation there is a movement from creation to new creation, from garden to garden and from tree of life to tree of life (Gen. 1–2; Rev. 21–22). This story starts "in the beginning" (Gen. 1:1) and goes from creation through the Fall into sin, with sin then spiraling and spilling out into the flood and the tower of Babel. It is in this aftermath that God calls Abraham and makes a covenant with the people of Israel. That story, however, ends in exile and unfulfillment. There is, however, a "yes and amen" (2 Cor. 1:20). The deep and final hope, redemption and re-creation, is found in Jesus Christ. He is the fulfillment and "it is finished" to God's promises (John 19:28), the "seed of the woman" (Gen. 3:15), the "offspring of Abraham" (Gal. 3:16), the descendant of David and "root of Jesse" (Rom. 1:3; 15:12). Jesus—Immanuel, "God with us" (Matt. 1:23)—comes to redeem and remake and restore and resurrect God's good creation and God's finite and fallen yet still forever loved people. After Jesus ascended, the Holy Spirit came and created the community that is the church, inaugurating the era between the earthly life and final return of Jesus. This promised and awaited coming is announced as new creation and consummation: the tree of life that was forfeit is forever replanted by the redeeming and re-creating love embodied on a tree of death. From creation to new creation by way of the crucified and risen Jesus. That is the scriptural story.

To summarize the Bible as story, however, is to leave a lot out. What do we do, for example, with Proverbs? Proverbs is not exactly part of the plotline. Proverbs contains and communicates some of the wisdom from God that Israel collected and shared. But Proverbs does not exactly or simply tell the story. Books like Psalms sometimes remember parts of the story, but these songs are more than story. They are also the prayerbook of Israel. What are the nature and roles of these books, and how do they give voice to the songs and praise, the wisdom and prayers of God's people now? Holy Scripture does more than narrate. As proverb and psalm, it instructs and prays; as poetry and prophecy, it provokes, questions, and addresses.

But even to summarize Holy Scripture as, in some fundamental sense, a single story, is to raise a crucial question: What—or better,

Martin Luther Preaching, predella of the Reformation Altar by Lucas Cranach the Elder (1472–1553), in the Stadtkirche St. Marien, Wittenberg, Germany

who—is the story finally and fundamentally about? Who is the subject of Holy Scripture?

A painting from the sixteenth century can help. Lucas Cranach was, among other things, an artist and collaborator with Martin Luther in the small university city of Wittenberg, Germany. In 1547, a year after Luther's death, Cranach produced an altarpiece for the town church that includes a central oil painting: *Martin Luther Preaching* (sometimes called the Reformation Altar and still in situ in the Stadtkirche St. Marien zu Wittenberg). When one studies the painting, a few essential details emerge.

There is a single and identifiable source for Luther's sermon. Standing in the pulpit, preaching and pointing, Luther is pictured with an open Bible. Holy Scripture is the source for the sermon. But what or who is the subject? At whom is Luther pointing and about whom is Luther preaching? Center stage: Christ crucified.

There is no hint or detail in the original painting that identifies whether the Bible is opened to Genesis, Deuteronomy, Psalms, Daniel, Mark, Romans, Hebrews, or Revelation. The image only indicates some page of the single source that is Holy Scripture. The artist, Lucas Cranach, with this detail—or lack of detail—is making a profound theological point: whatever passage a sermon speaks from, what the minister finally and only has to say and to give is always and only the crucified and risen Lord. As Paul reminds the Corinthians, what he preached was "the word of the cross," a message that is foolishness to the world and a stumbling block to those in Israel, but is, "to us," the "power and wisdom of God" (1 Cor. 1:18–25). This one "word of the cross," it seems, is Paul's single sermon: "I decided to know nothing among you except Jesus Christ and him crucified" (1 Cor. 2:2). Cranach's painting echoes Paul: whatever page or portion of Scripture Luther is preaching from, he is preaching and pointing to Jesus Christ.

This focus flows from Jesus's own testimony in the Gospels. In the last chapter of the Gospel according to Luke, Jesus encounters two disciples walking away from Jerusalem to a town called Emmaus. They are disappointed. They are despondent. They are in despair because Jesus has died and their hopes have therefore been dashed. At this moment—the moment of no hope that is so often the site of God's merciful surprise—the risen Jesus comes and walks with them, but they do not recognize him. Jesus asked, "What is this conversation you are having?" They reply, "Are you the only visitor to Jerusalem who does not know the things that have happened there?" The "things" they are referring to are the things "concerning Jesus" whom "[their] chief priest and rulers delivered up and condemned to death and crucified." "We had hoped," they lament, "he was the one to redeem Israel," but his crucifixion contradicts all that: no hope (Luke 24:12–21). Just here, at the point of honest confusion, fear, and need, Jesus speaks from the source—Holy Scripture—and speaks the only sermon: Jesus himself crucified and risen. "'How foolish you are, and how slow to believe all that the prophets have spoken! Did not the Messiah have to suffer these things and then enter his glory?' And beginning with Moses and all the Prophets, he explained to them what was said in all the Scriptures concerning himself" (AT). The entire Old Testament—"Moses and all the Prophets"—speaking about Jesus, revealing the needed and promised mercy of God in the suffering and saving Christ.

Two features of this scene stand out. One, the Old Testament—all of Holy Scripture—according to Jesus, is the story of Jesus and his death and his resurrection to redeem Israel and rescue the whole world. Two, the one who finally and fully reveals that story to these disciples is Jesus. Holy Scripture, it seems, both speaks about Jesus and is Jesus speaking. A fuller theological formulation might go like this: the Bible is the word of the God who is Father, Son, and Holy Spirit. Holy Scripture, as God's word, is the Father speaking in the power of the Holy Spirit to communicate and to give the Son.

A Christological focus follows from the way this God speaks in Scripture. As Jesus says to those who "search the Scriptures" in John 5:39–47, "If you believed Moses, you would believe me; for he wrote of me." As that gospel opens, "In the beginning was the Word, and the Word was with God, and the Word was God," and a few verses later, "the Word became flesh and dwelt among us" (John 1:1, 14). Jesus Christ, the Son of God, is the way God the Creator communes with and communicates to creation. "For the law was given through Moses; grace and truth came through Jesus Christ. No one has ever seen God; the only Son, who is at the Father's side, he has made him known" (1:17–18).

The Bible is the word of the God who is Father, Son, and Holy Spirit. Holy Scripture, as God's word, is the Father speaking in the power of the Holy Spirit to communicate and to give the Son.

The beginning of Hebrews puts it this way: "In many times and in many places, God has spoken through the prophets. But in these last days, he has spoken in his son" (Heb. 1:1–2, AT). This is God's final and definitive word to us. All God's speaking is gathered together in the "Word become flesh," promising and proclaiming who Jesus is and what he has done "for us and for our salvation" (Nicene Creed).

As Martin Luther sometimes said, however, it is one thing to find Jesus; it is another thing to "define" Jesus. To say Jesus is the subject of Holy Scripture is to pose the fundamental question: Who is Jesus Christ? This is a step toward the shape of Scripture. In Luther's words, "the highest art . . . is to define Christ . . . as the Son of God who . . . because of his sheer mercy and love, gave and offered himself for us." This Jesus, Luther seems to sing, "is not Moses . . . or a lawgiver; he is the dispenser of grace, the savior, the joy and sweetness of a trembling and troubled heart" (*Lectures on Galatians*). This definition includes others in Jesus's story, but as an "us" rather than an "I"—as those who are created and redeemed and loved by the God who in Christ is revealed as Creator, redeemer, and the one who is love (see, for example, John 1 and 1 John 4).

The Son of God is given two names in the opening chapter of the Gospel according to Matthew. The first name, in fulfillment of a prophecy from the Old Testament, is *Emmanuel*, which means "*God is with us*" (Matt. 1:23, quoting Isa. 7:14). This God that the Bible reveals, this Christ who comes to us and speaks to us about himself, is one who is with us. God does not remain far off. God comes to us. Whether this "God with us" is good news, however, depends entirely on who this God is. In Greek mythology, for instance, when a god came among mortals, a "god with us" was haunting rather than hopeful news. The one Matthew calls Emmanuel, however, is also the one that he calls Jesus. That name—Yeshua or Joshua or Jesus—means: "He will save you from your sins" (Matt. 1:21, AT).

The God who is *with* us is also and fundamentally the God who is *for* us. The story about Jesus, because it is about the God who is with us and for us, is also our story, the story of those whom God is *with*, those whom God is *for*. This is our story—our life and our salvation: those God creates because God loves, those God wills to be with because God loves, those God forgives because this God will finally and forever love. Question 1 of the Heidelberg Catechism asks, "What is your only comfort in life and death?" The response: "That I am not my own but belong, with body and soul, both in life and in death, to my faithful savior Jesus Christ."

Holy Scripture talks about both the Creator and creation, but it never mixes the two up. God is God: "Hear, O Israel, the LORD your God, the LORD is one," and "You shall have no other gods before him" (Deut. 6:4, AT; 5:7, AT). In Revelation 4–5, God and the Lamb are "worthy," whereas all that is "in heaven or on earth or under the earth" is "not worthy" (Rev. 4:11; 5:2–4, 12). It is this God, however, the one who is always and eternally and by nature God, who in freedom, love, and grace creates and comes. This God is the one who brought you out of the land of Egypt (Exod. 20:2), who raised Jesus Christ from the dead (Rom. 4:24), who "so loved the world, that he gave his only Son so that all who believe in him will not perish but have everlasting life" (John 3:16, AT). It is this God who speaks in Scripture and says, "As far as the east is from the west, so far have I removed your sins from you" (Ps. 103:12, AT).

Holy Scripture is God speaking and revealing God to us in the life, death, and resurrection of Jesus. This speaking and this story, however, is also our story, the revelation of who we are, the unearthing of our honest need, and the giving of the one who wipes away each tear, sets the captive free, forgives sin, and resurrects the dead. As Paul says in Romans 8:39, "I'm convinced that nothing in all creation can separate us from the love of God that is in Christ Jesus" (AT). From beginning to end, this is a story of a God who loves even those who are in rebellion, who loves those who cannot restore or redeem themselves. God's love is stronger than sin, stronger than death, and nothing and no one can separate us from it. This is the relationship God will have with the creation he "so loved" (John 3:16).

This relationship is not only remembered or recorded in Holy Scripture. Because this "word of God" is "living and active" (Heb. 4:12), God speaking in Scripture to those who hear and read is a form and occurrence of this relationship. God speaks, we hear, and this is real relationship with the living God. Perhaps the Bible should have one of those warning labels albums sometimes have (or at least used to have). In the case of Holy Scripture, the warning is less a matter of "explicit lyrics" (though there is plenty of that);

the peril—and the promise—is effective or even explosive lyrics. Hebrews calls divine speech the "living and active" word (Heb. 4:12), a reminder that, in Luther's phrase, God's word is "a word of reality" that does what it says (*Lecture on Psalm 2*). "In the beginning," according to Genesis, "God said, 'Let there be light,' and there was light" (Gen. 1:3). This pattern is present in Jesus's life, as his command is reality creating and his promise performs the impossible. At the bedside of a dead girl and the tomb of Lazarus, Jesus commands, "Little girl, get up" (Mark 5:41, AT) and "Lazarus, come out" (John 11:43), and death is overcome by the word of grace that opens up the grave.

Some in the sixteenth century liked to say that God's word is two words: an address to the fallen that reveals human need and an announcement that speaks at the site of sin and death and, in Jesus's name, forgives and makes alive. Luther's colleague Philip Melanchthon calls these "two words" the "two works of God," emphasizing the creative power and merciful purpose of divine speech (*Apology of the Augsburg Confession*). This means that the word of God spoken in Holy Scripture is not only information or instruction. It is God's action. To attend to this address, to hear the sound of divine speech—to read the Bible—is to undergo the action of God, whose word creates and resurrects. This entails turning upside down some assumptions about reading the Bible. It is perhaps natural to think that I open this book, I read the Bible, and therefore I interpret Holy Scripture. But because this is the "living and active" word (Heb. 4:12) of the one who "spoke, and it came to be" (Ps. 33:9), it is God who is at work and we who are being addressed and acted upon. The Bible does not so much sit there waiting to be inter-

> *The Bible does not so much sit there waiting to be interpreted. The reality of reading is that God speaks and acts so that we are interpreted by Scripture. It is less true that we read the Bible; it is truer that the Bible reads us.*

Law and Gospel, by Lucas Cranach the Elder (1472–1553)

preted. The reality of reading is that God speaks and acts so that we are interpreted by Scripture. It is less true that we read the Bible; it is truer that the Bible reads us.

Another image that came out of Lucas Cranach's workshop illustrates the power and shape of God's creative and living word. Cranach, and later his son, produced a few versions of a diptych portraying the two words (or two works) of God under the title *Law and Gospel*. The oil-on-wood painting from 1529 is a stunning example, and it suggestively pairs image and scriptural texts. Consider, however, this woodcut from 1530.

The scene is divided into two, with a tree cutting through the middle. There is that story again. From a tree of life in an original garden in Genesis to a restored tree of life in the new garden of Revelation by way of Jesus's death on a tree: a tree of death that is the site and source of life for all. This image, however, with its dividing line, not only tells a story; it indicates a shape. The tree is barren on one side but in bloom on the other. On both sides, there is the same human person, a figure meant to represent all human beings, someone like Adam or Eve—the human. The drama depicts what happens to human beings when they are addressed by God. All the imagery and all the details in the woodcut are scenes or stories from the Bible. As those things—those words of God—are encountered, something happens to the human. This is not isolated and unaffected study. The human person is not only learning about the Fall, Moses giving the law, final judgment, or the death and resurrection of Jesus. These words are doing something, they are "living and active." As Moses points to and proclaims the law, sin and death reign and the human person is driven to fear and condemnation. On the other side, John the Baptist points to and proclaims not "the law" that "was given through Moses" but the "grace and truth" that is the crucified and risen Christ (John 1:17). His sermon, to quote John 1:29, is always and only, "Behold, the Lamb of God, who takes away the sin of the world!" This news, announced in the word and present to the human person in the dove that is the descent of the Holy Spirit, appears to bring peace, hope, and rest where before there was only fear, shame, and sin. This promise is the hope of the whole Bible, as the scene from Israel's wilderness wanderings in Numbers suggests (see the tents in the background). And it is this promise—the gospel of Jesus Christ—that speaks at the site of captivity, fear, need, and death and gives Jesus, who sets free, brings peace, forgives, and makes alive.

There are passages in Holy Scripture where this panoramic action of God through the word is summarized and celebrated. Among the most beautiful is 1 Samuel 2. Hannah, the mother of Samuel, is dedicating her son. As she does so, she sings a song that traces the character—the ways and the works—of God. In the words of Hannah's song,

> "The Lord kills and brings to life;
>   he brings down to Sheol and raises up.

> The LORD makes poor and makes rich;
> he brings low and he exalts." (1 Sam. 2:6–7)

God is doing two things in Hannah's song. There is a shape and sequence, an order and a horizon. First, God brings down to Sheol, down to death. God humbles and makes poor. But then, out of the ashes and from the dead, God raises up and brings to life. God exalts and makes rich.

Mary sings a similar song. Her "soul magnifies the Lord"; she sings of "God my savior," who acts "in remembrance of his mercy." This God "scatters the proud" and "brings down the mighty," but in "his mercy" God has "exalted those of humble estate" and "filled the hungry with good things" (Luke 1:46–55, AT). The word of the Lord—in Genesis and the Gospels, in Numbers and Jude, from Ruth to Revelation—acts in this double and with-direction way: God unearths deep and real human need, and then God, in the gospel, gives Jesus who is, as 1 Corinthians 1:30 says, "the source of your life" and "our wisdom and our righteousness and sanctification and redemption" (AT). In Paul's summary, "The Lord has imprisoned all in disobedience in order that he might have mercy on all" (Rom. 11:32, AT). A double work linked by an "in order that." God imprisoned all in disobedience. This was so that God might have mercy on all. Again, twofold and with a telos: revealed and honest need; promised and given mercy through Jesus Christ. If God's word first works to occasion an honest cry, "Who will deliver me?" God's final work is a "comfortable word," "There is therefore now no condemnation for those who are in Christ Jesus" (Rom. 7:24; 8:1). God speaks to reveal need for Jesus. God speaks to give Jesus.

Revelation 5 is a scene that summarizes the themes of this chapter. The word "revelation" means to unveil, and as the curtain parts, the reader of Revelation is invited to see what is real. Revelation is a summons, "come here" and "behold" (4:1). What is first revealed as what is fundamentally real is God, on the throne and ceaselessly worshiped. "Holy, holy, holy, is the Lord God Almighty" (Rev. 4:8).

This refrain is reality. In Revelation 5, however, this first and fundamental reality reveals another: that God is God entails that we are not. This is unveiled as a "strong angel" asks, "Who is worthy to open the scroll" held by the "Holy, holy, holy" Lord? (4:8; 5:2). The conclusion comes: "no one in heaven or on earth or under the earth was able to open to scroll or to look into it" (5:3). Faced with this bedrock fact, John the Seer says, "I began to weep" (5:4).

This is unveiled honesty in the presence of the holy God. "Worthy are you, our Lord and God" uncovers the "no one was found worthy" of honest human finitude and need (4:11; 5:4). But weeping is not the last word. As the tears still soak the Seer's eyes, another creature comes along. This can only be another among the unworthy. Only God is God and therefore all, John saw, in heaven, on earth, and under the earth are grouped in total solidarity: the universal league of the unworthy. But this creature comes with a comfortable word: "Weep no more; behold, the Lion of the tribe of Judah, the Root of David, has conquered" (5:5). This unworthy but compassionate witness points away from himself and to the Lion. John looked, and behold: "I saw a Lamb standing, as though it had been slain" (5:6). This Lamb "went and took the scroll," and suddenly there is a new song,

> "Worthy are you . . .
> for you were slain, and by your blood you ransomed
> people for God
> from every tribe and language and people and
> nation." (5:7–9)

The song swells, and all those who were unworthy become those who worship: "every creature in heaven and on earth and under the earth and in the sea" sings "worthy is the Lamb" (5:12–13).

This sequence is both a story within Holy Scripture and the story of all of Holy Scripture. God is God and we are not. "Worthy are you, our Lord and God" is a word that reveals, irrespective of pedigree or performance, "no one is worthy." This unearthed honesty can be a time for tears. But again, weeping is not the final word. That word, in solidarity and sympathy, is "weep no more." This is no "cruel optimism" or denial of the sorrow and sin that haunt human life. This word is spoken by those whose own tears have salted the earth. But this word, like the finger of John the Baptist, says, behold: the slain Lamb is the one who "will wipe away every tear from their eyes, and death shall be no more, neither shall there be mourning, nor crying, nor pain anymore." This is the promise of "the living one," the one who says, "I died, and behold I am alive forevermore" (Rev. 1:18). In this "Son of God, who loved me and gave himself for me" (Gal. 2:20), the unworthy go from weeping to worship: "Worthy is the Lamb."

PART 1

The Old Testament

CHAPTER 1

The Law (Torah)

"HEAR, O ISRAEL: The LORD our God, the LORD is one" (Deut. 6:4). This one Lord is the God who "in the beginning . . . created the heavens and the earth" (Gen. 1:1), the one who is "the God of Abraham, the God of Isaac, and the God of Jacob" (Exod. 3:15). It is this Lord, the God of creation and covenant, who says to Israel, "I am the LORD your God, who brought you out of the land of Egypt, out of the house of slavery. You shall have no other gods before me" (Exod. 20:2–3). The history of Israel, however, includes "chasing after idols" (Jer. 2:25, AT; Ps. 16:4), and exodus from Egypt gives way to exile from Israel. The question posed is whether exile is the end: "Can these bones live?" (Ezek. 37:3). The final answer is promised: "Behold, I will open your graves and raise you from your graves, O my people. And I will bring you into the land of Israel. And you shall know that I am the LORD, when I open your graves" (Ezek. 37:12–13). Because the Lord is this God—the Creator and redeemer and grave-opener—"death is not the end" (Bob Dylan).

—

The Old Testament can be divided into three groups of writings. Christians refer to this collection of writings as the Old Testament. The Jewish name for what Christians call the Old Testament is the

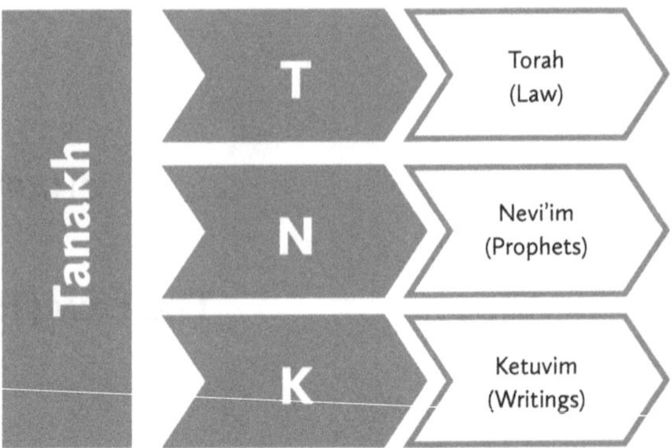

Tanakh. Tanakh is a Hebrew acronym for the three parts of this collection of writings. The *T* stands for "Torah," or the Law, the first five books. The *N* is the Nevi'im, the Prophets. The *K* in "Tanakh" is "Ketuvim," which is the Writings. The Tanakh is the Torah, Nevi'im, and Ketuvim, the Law, the Prophets, and the Writings. The next three chapters follow this threefold partition of the Old Testament starting with the Torah, which is often referred to as the Pentateuch, or "five books": Genesis, Exodus, Leviticus, Numbers, and Deuteronomy.

"In the beginning God" (Gen. 1:1). The opening words of Holy Scripture confess that God is. When asked for the divine name by Moses, God says, "I am and will be who I am and will be" (Exod. 3:14, AT). The first sentence of Scripture, however, says not only "God" but "God created the heavens and the earth." Because God was, is, and will be, the divine life has no lack. God is, and so God acts not from necessity or need but only from freedom and love. God is, and it is by grace that God wills to be God with and for creation. As Martin Luther says in the *Small Catechism*, "God created me together with all that exists . . . all this is done out of pure, fatherly, and divine goodness and mercy, without any merit or worthiness of mine." God creates not out of need but from nothing: all that is only is by the mercy, love, and grace of God.

The stories of the Torah, the accounts of creation and covenant, are stories of God and God's grace. The Torah offers a narrative that runs from creation to the calling of Abraham, and from the exodus to the covenant with Israel. Genesis offers accounts of creation, the emergence of sin and death, the flood, the tower of Babel, the call of Abraham, and the generations of his family. Exodus opens with Israel in Egypt, a bondage from which God through Moses delivers them. The freed descendants of Abraham who pass through the Red Sea receive the law on Sinai, which is recorded in Exodus and Leviticus, and rearticulated in Deuteronomy. Mount Sinai, in both geographic and literary terms, is the center of the Torah, and it is here that God renews the covenant and announces again the promises of land and life. Forty years of wandering in the wilderness, much of which is recounted in Numbers, end with Israel on the edge: brought to the border of but not yet in the promised land, having heard afresh God's promise of life but still in a wilderness that has been a "shadow of death" (Ps. 23).

This sense of almost and anticipation is a motif in the Old Testament. There is movement, and the promise has not failed, but the fulfillment is still on the horizon. The promises hold, but they hold as hope. There is a pattern in the Old Testament, a promise that stands but seems to stop on the cusp of the hoped-for. At the end of Deuteronomy, which is the end of the Pentateuch, the reader stands on the edge: from an elevated region Moses looks upon the longed-for land. "Almost," the scene seems to whisper, but it is still there rather than here.

The end of the Torah offers a good beginning. The book of Deuteronomy provides a shape or pattern that is often present in Genesis, Exodus, Leviticus, and Numbers. This pattern is explicit near the end of the book: "If you fully obey the voice of the Lord your God, and carefully follow all his commandments which I give you today, the Lord your God will set you high above all nations of the earth, then all these blessings will come upon you and accompany you, because you obey the voice of the Lord your God" (Deut. 28:1–2, AT). If you obey the Lord, you will have these blessings. That is one half of the pattern in Deuteronomy: obey, bless-

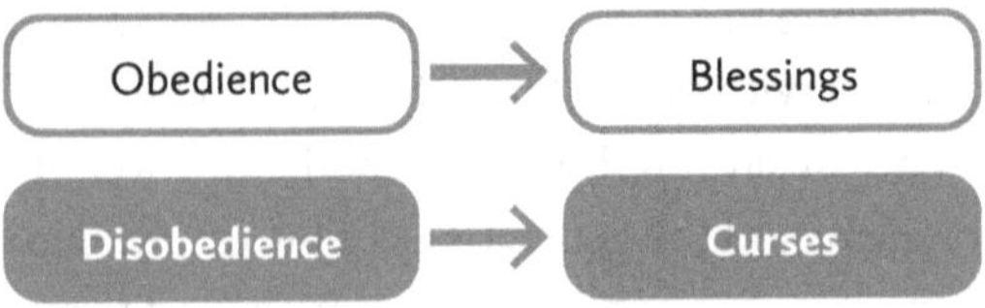

ings. The second half of the pattern is given in Deuteronomy 28:15: "However, if you do not obey the voice of the LORD your God and do not carefully follow all his commandments and his statutes that I command you today, then all these curses shall come upon you and overtake you" (AT).

This pattern of obedience leading to blessing and disobedience leading to curses is crucial, not just for Deuteronomy but also for the shape of the Torah and all Holy Scripture. This is sometimes called the "Deuteronomic pattern": if you obey, blessing; if you disobey, curse. In Deuteronomy, however, this apparently symmetrical calculus of blessing and curse is not the final word. Moses ends his instructions with a stark warning that is also a promise. "All these curses will come upon you" (Deut. 28:45, AT) and "the LORD will drive you . . . to a nation unknown to you" (28:36, AT). About to enter the land, hearing again the pattern and promise of blessing and curse, the people on the edge of the land are told they will be exiled from it: "these curses will come." The disobedience Moses foretells becomes a description of the history of Israel and Judah as narrated in 1 and 2 Kings. Exile does occur, the curses do come.

But then God, through Moses, makes a promise: even exile is not the end. There is a promise beyond the pattern, a grace greater than the calculus of blessing and curse: "Even if you have been banished to the most distant land under the heavens, from there the LORD your God will gather you and bring you back. He will bring you to the land that belonged to your ancestors, and you will take possession of it. He will make you more prosperous and numerous than your ancestors" (Deut. 30:4–5, AT). Exile is not the end. There is a blessing beyond the curse. There is mercy beyond judgment.

There is life beyond and out of death. That is the deep and final pattern—the final promise—of Deuteronomy.

This is the bedrock question posed by the Torah: Is God's promise stronger than disobedience and death? God made a promise to Noah, Moses, Abraham, Isaac, Jacob, and to the people of Israel, but the question is, Do disobedience and death—and there is significant death in the Pentateuch, including a whole generation in Numbers—finally undo and defeat God's promise? Or is God's promise stronger than disobedience and stronger than death? Are there hope and mercy even on the other side of the curses? Is there, by grace, life even after and out of the grave? Perhaps, as Paul writes in Romans 11:32, "God consigned all in disobedience," but does God's mercy mean forgiveness for the disobedient and life even for the dead? The promise of the Pentateuch is: yes. God's mercy and love are stronger than death, stronger than disobedience, and yet—and yet—the final form and fulfillment of this mercy is still on the horizon—it is hope.

Before that end, however, the beginning: Genesis.

Genesis is divided into two basic parts. Genesis 1–11 tells the origins and the early history of the whole world, meaning a history of everyone and everything. "In the beginning, God created the heavens and the earth." That God creates the sea, sky, and land and also all that lives within them announces a distinction between Creator and creature: other ancient peoples might worship the sun and stars or the beasts and birds, but these and everything else are good yet not-god creatures of the one who "in the beginning created." The creation accounts of Genesis 1–2 in which "it was good" (1:9) give way to the entrance of sin and death in Genesis 3. From there the story is a spiral of sin: Cain kills Abel (Gen. 4), the flood occurs when "the thoughts of the human heart were only evil all the time" (6:5, AT), the inhabits of Babel attempt "a tower that reaches to the heavens" (11:4, AT). The ambition under this architecture is an inversion of the first commandment: "I am the Lord your God" is contradicted by the Eden-old "you will be like God" (Gen. 3:5). "Let us build . . . a tower," they say, "so that we may make a name for

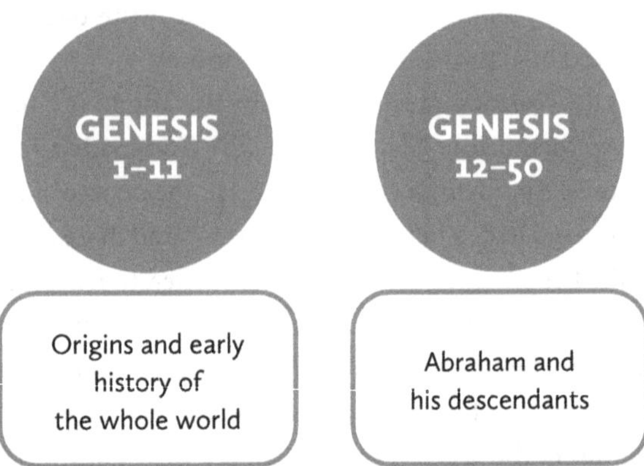

ourselves" (11:4, AT). But "the LORD came down" (11:5), a reminder that to be a human creature is not to climb to God but to live from the grace of the God who creates and comes to us.

Something shifts in Genesis 12. The focus on all creation narrows to Abraham and God's covenant. In Genesis 12, God calls Abraham—named Abram at this stage of the story—and God makes a promise: "I will make you into a great nation, and I will bless you and make your name great . . . and in you all the families of the earth will be blessed" (12:1–3, AT). The rest of Genesis, chapters 12–50, is the story of Abraham and the family of Abraham: his wife, Sarah, and their son, Isaac, Isaac's wife, Rebekah, and their son Jacob, who eventually fathered twelve sons who become the touchstones for the twelve tribes of Israel.

To read Genesis is to feel the tension between God as the "God of Abraham, Isaac, and Jacob" and this same and single God as the God who "in the beginning created the heavens and the earth." Understanding Genesis entails being attuned to the double scope: the God of Israel is also the God of all. The prophets declare again and again that the God of Abraham—the God who brought Israel out of Egypt—is not *a* lord but *the* Lord. Unlike other local or tribal deities that are finally idols, this God is both more powerful than the gods of Egypt or Canaan or Babylon and also, from the beginning and in the end, the only God. "I am the LORD your God" and "you shall have no other gods" (Exod. 20:2–3). "Hear, O Israel: The LORD our God, the LORD is one" (Deut. 6:4).

In the New Testament, the tension between Genesis 1–11 and Genesis 12–50 comes together in Jesus Christ: through Israel and through the one Israelite Jesus of Nazareth, God both fulfills the promises to Israel and redeems the whole world. Even in Genesis, however, chapters 1–11 and 12–50 are linked by a pattern of divine action. God, in both creation and covenant, acts to call into existence and call into covenant that which neither is nor is deserving.

In creation, God is not compelled by any lack in the divine life. "In the beginning, God." And yet, "In the beginning, God created." This, again, is not from necessity or need but from nothing: God, in freedom and love, calls into the chaos, and there is creation. This first act reveals the fundament of all God's acts: God was and is and will be the God of grace. God acts for our good, not because we are good but rather because God is good and gracious. There is a kind of rhyme between creation and redemption: God acts, first and finally and forever, by grace.

"By grace" is the shape of Genesis. Adam and Eve are called into life, not out of divine lack but from the overflow of God's love (Gen. 1–2). After Adam and Eve fall (Gen. 3), there is judgment—"In pain you shall bring forth children" (3:16) and "cursed is the ground" (3:17)—but there is also provision and promise: "the LORD God made for Adam and for his wife garments of skin and clothed them" (3:21), and to the serpent it is said that "the seed of the women will bruise [its] head" (3:15, AT). God made clothes for them to cover their shame and nakedness. In the wake of Cain's murder of Abel, God's question to Cain—"Where is Abel your brother?"—evokes a fear of deserved death—"whoever finds me will kill me"— that is met with surprising mercy: "Not so" (4:8–15).

God acts for our good, not because we are good but rather because God is good and gracious.

The flood follows the same pattern. It is when "every intention of the thoughts of human hearts was only evil all the time" (6:5, AT) that "Noah found favor in the eyes of the LORD" (6:8). The flood itself is a severe instance of judgment, and yet out of this second watery chaos God, again and in mercy, creates. The story of the tower of Babel reveals a similarly universal sinfulness. And yet, in the aftermath of God's judgment comes a word of God's grace: "Now the LORD said to Abram, 'Go,'" and "I will make of you a great nation" (12:1–2). The absence of any backstory that suggests the distinctive worthiness of Abraham is an indication that he, like all, was among the idolatrous. But at the site of sin, God acts in grace. As Paul says of Abraham in Romans 4:5, "He trusted the one who justifies the ungodly" (AT). This is a refrain in Genesis, and as Deuteronomy 7:6–8 proclaims, grace is Israel's bedrock: "The LORD your God has chosen you to be a people for his treasured possession. . . . It was not because you were more in number than any other people . . . for you were the fewest of all peoples, but it is because the LORD loves you."

Another motif in Genesis that reflects this pattern of forgiving and life-giving grace is barrenness. In Genesis 15, God commands Abraham to "number the stars" and then says, "So shall your offspring be" (15:5). This is an impossible promise: Abraham is a hundred years old, and Sarah is ninety and barren. When this promise is spoken again in Genesis 17, the absurdity causes Abraham to laugh (17:17). This first laugher, however, is not the final laughter. Out of aged bodies and barren wombs, God brings the miracle of life. As Genesis 21:1 records, "the LORD did . . . as he had promised." This is a promise beyond the possible, and Abraham's laughter is replaced by Sarah's, who names her son Isaac—Joy or Laughter—and says, "God has made laughter for me; everyone who hears will laugh over me" (21:3–6).

The next generation in Genesis is also haunted by barrenness. But by now, mercy has become the divine motif: it is where there is not and cannot be life that God, by grace, gives life. The God who, into the darkness, said, "Let there be light," is also and always the God who, at the site of barrenness and death, says, "Let there be life."

The paradigmatic episode of God's mercy at the point of no hope is the exodus. This event of divine deliverance is fundamental to the identification both of Israel and of Israel's Lord. At the end of Genesis, Joseph and his brothers, the sons of Jacob, are in Egypt. As Exodus opens, however, "there arose a new king over Egypt, who did not know Joseph" (Exod. 1:8). The people of Israel are enslaved by the Egyptians, set to impossible tasks (making bricks without straw, 5:10) and experiencing horrific suffering (Pharaoh's order to kill the Hebrew newborn boys, 1:16). Israel is at its most hopeless, the moment at which God's promises seem impossible. But, as God says to Moses from the burning bush, "I have surely seen the affliction of my people who are in Egypt and have heard their cry. . . . I know their sufferings, and I have come down to deliver them" (Exod. 3:7–8).

Exodus plays out this story as a contest between the God of Abraham, Isaac, and Jacob, and Pharaoh and the gods of Egypt. At every point, Pharaoh and the gods of Egypt are exposed as pretenders, rivals, and nothing but idols who are powerless and impotent in the face of the one true God, who not only called the world into being but is now calling Israel out of Egypt. Just as God called and created, so too God is calling and setting free. It is an act of the Creator's power that delivers Israel from bondage and suffering. This is seen in nature plagues, for example, the frogs and flies and the Nile turned to blood (Exod. 7–8). But the central drama of this deliverance is the revelation of God's power over life and death (the Passover, Exod. 12) and the parting of the Red Sea (Exod. 14). It is the God whose name is "I AM WHO I AM" (3:14) that brought Israel out of Egypt and brought Israel to Mount Sinai. Here "the LORD, the God of your fathers, the God of Abraham, the God of Isaac, and the God of Jacob," calls himself "the LORD your God, who brought you out of the land of Egypt" (20:2).

But there is still a problem in the story: Israel has been set free and commanded to "have no other gods" before God (20:3), but this once suffering-and-enslaved and now set-free people are, in some basic sense, still the same. Exodus, as it transpires, does not equal the elimination of sin and suffering. The children of Abraham are still the children of Adam and Eve. Much of Leviticus, for example, describes how these unholy people could be and could become God's holy people. Leviticus outlines the laws and regulations for how they should live in the presence of the holy God. This ranges from how to worship in the sanctuary to how to interact with neighbors, how to buy livestock, or what to do when an outsider comes among the people. Leviticus provides a comprehensive vision of how to be the holy people of the holy God. Yet built into the Levitical codes—as a fundamental feature rather than an inconvenient bug—is the system of sacrifice. Sacrifice faces the facts: the people who are called to be holy before God are not holy. At the center of the book of Leviticus is the Day of Atonement, the annual day of sacrifice for the sins of the people (Lev. 16). Life with the holy God entails a love that forgives and a mercy that restores. The provision and practices of the Day of Atonement—with the blood of bulls and goats and the holy place where God is present in mercy—whisper a promise: forgiveness will be forever because one sacrifice will be final. As Hebrews proclaims, "Every priest stands daily at his service, offering repeatedly the same sacrifices, which can never take away sins. But when Christ had offered for all time a single sacrifice for sins, he sat down" (Heb. 10:11–12).

This tension between the promised communion with and the categorical difference between the holy God and the still-human people plays out dramatically in Exodus and Numbers. Exodus 19–20 and Exodus 32–34 narrate the accounts of the giving of the law. Moses ascends Mount Sinai to receive the tablets of the Ten Commandments and then comes down to deliver them to the people. The scene is programmatic: What happens when the holy law is heard by human people?

Moses declares the law of the Lord: "I am the LORD your God. . . . You shall have no other gods. . . . You shall not make for yourself a carved image, or any likeness" (Exod. 20:1–4). While

Moses is on the mountain, however, the people are also speaking: "these"—the golden calf Israel has just made—"these are your gods, O Israel" (32:4). This contrast between God's law and Israel's life results in death: "three thousand men of the people fell" and "the LORD sent a plague on the people, because they made the calf" (32:28, 35). Paul refers to this episode in 2 Corinthians and calls the law, "carved in letters on stone," a "ministry of death" (2 Cor. 3:7). The law is, as Paul also says, "holy and righteous and good" (Rom. 7:12), but its perfect holiness and righteousness and goodness are "not," in Francis Spufford's words, "sized for human life" (*Unapologetic*). "The law of God," which Martin Luther calls "the most salutary doctrine of life, cannot advance a person on the way to righteousness" (*Heidelberg Disputation*). God's good law, addressed to the finite and fallen people of Israel, does not eliminate Israel's idolatry and continued need; the law, rather, exposes and identifies Israel's idolatry and need.

If the dramatic account of this is the giving of the law, the extended version is the book of Numbers. Numbers opens with, and near the end includes, numbers: censuses of the people of Israel. The first list identifies the generation that God delivered out of Egypt. The second list, in Numbers 26, is again the people of Israel, but this one lists a new generation prepared to enter the promised land. The startling and significant detail contained in these censuses is this: the two lists do not overlap. Those who had been in Egypt, those whom God delivered, are dead. Among those whom Moses sent to spy out the land, only Caleb and Joshua are permitted by God to enter, and it is Joshua who is "commissioned" to succeed Moses (Num. 27:12–23).

Between the two numberings of the people, the book of Numbers tells the history of the first generation of Israel living in covenant with, and under the law of, God. The death that accompanied the giving and immediate violation of the law haunts the history of Numbers. In one passage, the earth "opened its mouth and swallowed them up, with their households" (16:32). At another point, "parts of the camp" are "consumed" by "the fire of the LORD" (11:1). The intimate nearness yet fundamental distance between the one holy God and the only human people plays out as rebellion, disobedience, judgment, and death. A generation of life under the law exposes Israel's persistent idolatry and renders a diagnosis as deep as death. The promised land is only possible as promise: not Israel's obedience and faithfulness but only the mercy and faithfulness of God.

Numbers poses the question of the Torah. Do disobedience and death disqualify Israel from and defeat God's promise? At the end of Numbers, the exodus generation is dead. Moses is not to enter the land. God's promise is unfulfilled. But has it failed? The question in Numbers is, Which is final—disobedience and death, or God and grace? The answer, both "in the beginning" and even after exile, is God and grace. "In the beginning, God," and after the end, "the LORD your God will bring you back" (Deut. 30:5, AT).

CHAPTER 2

The Prophets (Nevi'im)

THE PROPHETS. This is the second section of the Old Testament, the Nevi'im. The collection of prophetic literature includes obviously prophetic books such as Isaiah, Jeremiah, and Ezekiel but also more historical or narrative books including Joshua, Judges, and the books of Samuel and Kings. Prophets, as a name for a part of the Old Testament, collects together two kinds of texts: historical and prophetic. The historical books recount the history of Israel from their entrance into the promised land under Joshua up to and beyond exile. This includes conquest, the era of the judges, a united monarchy under David and Solomon, and the division of the kingdom into Israel in the north and Judah in the south. Israel is conquered and scattered by the Assyrians in 722 BC. Judah is defeated and exiled by the Babylonians in 586 BC (after an initial deportation in 596 BC).

The prophetic literature can also be classified with the distinction between former and latter prophets. The are those who are active before the division of the kingdom; the latter prophets speak their oracles after the division, up to and often in exile. Elijah, Elisha, and Nathan (who was a prophet to King David) are among the former prophets. The latter prophets include Isaiah, Ezekiel, Jeremiah, and the Book of the Twelve minor prophets. (Daniel, while a prophetic book, is traditionally placed within the Writings, or Ketuvim.)

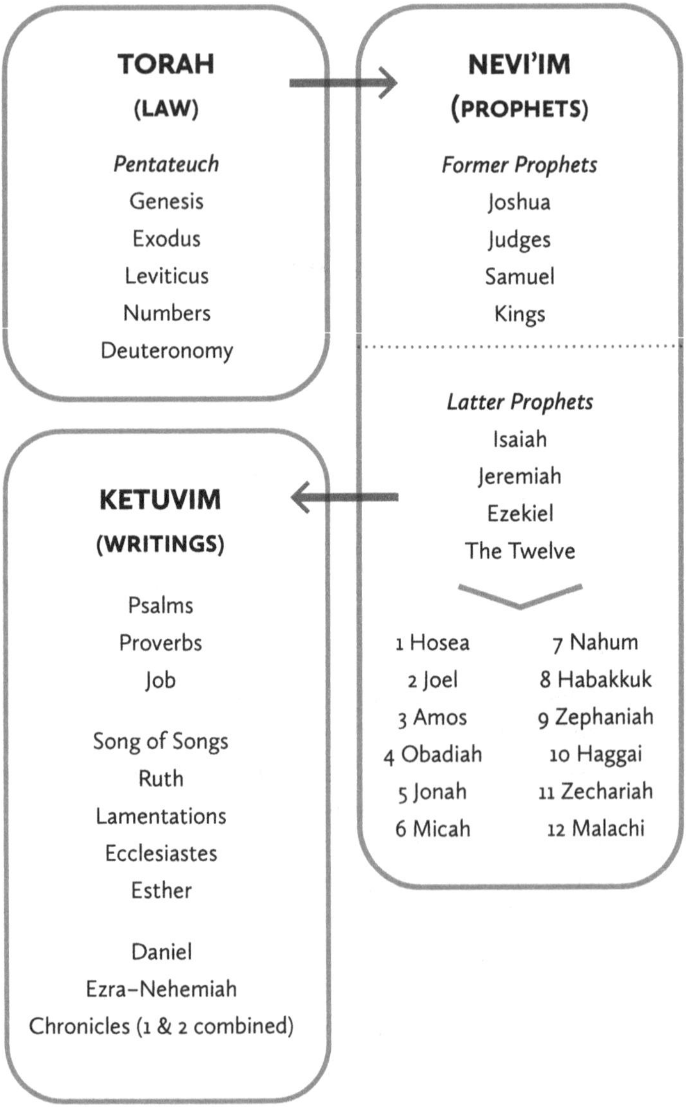

TORAH
(LAW)

Pentateuch
Genesis
Exodus
Leviticus
Numbers
Deuteronomy

NEVI'IM
(PROPHETS)

Former Prophets
Joshua
Judges
Samuel
Kings

Latter Prophets
Isaiah
Jeremiah
Ezekiel
The Twelve

1 Hosea	7 Nahum
2 Joel	8 Habakkuk
3 Amos	9 Zephaniah
4 Obadiah	10 Haggai
5 Jonah	11 Zechariah
6 Micah	12 Malachi

KETUVIM
(WRITINGS)

Psalms
Proverbs
Job

Song of Songs
Ruth
Lamentations
Ecclesiastes
Esther

Daniel
Ezra–Nehemiah
Chronicles (1 & 2 combined)

THE BOOKS OF
TANAKH

FORMER PROPHETS	**LATTER PROPHETS**
History **before** the divided kingdom. Provide **context** for the prophecies.	**After** the kingdom divided (during exile). Provide **content** of the prophecies.
Joshua	Isaiah
Judges	Ezekiel
1–2 Samuel	Jeremiah
1–2 Kings	Book of the Twelve

The historical books, which offer their own distinctive witness as prophetic history, tell the story of Israel in the promised land from entrance to exile. The movements and moments in this history—judges, united monarchy, divided kingdom, exile—are the contexts within which the former and latter prophets speak and act. This holds the history and prophecies together. As the voices of the prophets are presented in the biblical canon, the historical books provide the *context* in which the prophets spoke; the prophetic books provide the *content* that the prophets spoke (see *Engaging the Christian Scriptures*). The words of a prophet match a historical moment. Amos, for instance, addresses the northern kingdom of Israel as it is about to fall to Assyria.

This dual reading, because it locates the prophets in the history of Israel, is a reminder that the "thus says the Lord" of the prophets addresses concrete situations. The prophets are not just strange oracles speaking in a timeless void; they offer particular, pastoral, prophetic words of judgment and grace for real and specific moments in Israel's history. A prophet, in the most basic sense, is one who speaks for God. The words a prophet speaks (or writes or enacts) are as various as the concrete word God gives and the specific context they address. Prophecy often connotes something predictive, suggesting that pro-

Approximate Date	Judah	Israel	Prophet
922-900 BC	Rehoboam, Abijah Asa	Jeroboam	
900-850 BC	Jehoshaphat	Nadab, Bassha, Elah, Zimri, Omri, Ahab	Elijah (Israel)
850-800	Jehoram, Ahaziah, Athaliah, Joash	Ahaziah, Jehoram, Jehu, Jehoahaz	Elisha (Israel)
800-750	Amaziah, Uzziah	Jehoash, Jerebo-am II	Amos (Israel)
750-700	Jotham, Ahaz	Zechariah, Shal-lum, Menahem, Pekahiah, Pekah, Hoshea Fall of Israel to the Assyrians	Hosea (Israel) Isaiah (Judah) Micah (Judah)
700-650	Hezekiah, Manasseh		
650-600	Amon, Josi-ah, Jehoahaz, Jehoiakim		Jeremiah Zephaniah Nahum
600-530	Jehoiachin, Zedekiah Fall of Jerusalem to Babylon and Exile		Habakkuk Ezekiel

The Rulers and Prophets of Judah and Israel

phetic words are a foretelling. This future orientation is certainly part of the prophetic literature of Holy Scripture, especially in the form of warning and promise. A prophet, however, is not first or fundamentally one who foretells but rather one who forth-tells. Prophets speak forth the message God has given them. As the book of Joel opens, "The word of the LORD that came to Joel" (Joel 1:1). The prophetic genre is defined by divine address: "thus says the LORD." For this reason, in contexts of division, idolatry, and injustice, the prophets are rarely popular, especially among the powerful.

Reading the historical books alongside the books of the prophets also indicates that the biblical prophets were not the only people styling themselves "prophets" throughout Israel's history. First Kings 18 dramatizes a contest between "prophets of Baal" and Elijah. Or consider Jeremiah, for example, who announces God's coming judgment, the imminence of exile, and only then a promised return and redemption. As Jeremiah delivers God's word of judgment, there are false prophets in Jerusalem whose "prophecy" makes the opposite promise: "They dress the wound of my people lightly," says the Lord through Jeremiah, with their false promise of "'Peace, peace,' when there is no peace" (Jer. 6:14, AT). Against the popular life of imagined peace, Jeremiah speaks the truth. This is what it is to be a prophet: to say what God has shown and spoken, whether that is "the vision of Obadiah" (Obad. 1), "the word of the LORD that came to Micah" or "to Hosea" (Mic. 1:1; Hosea 1:1), or "the oracle of the word of the LORD to Israel by Malachi" (Mal. 1:1). This "word of the LORD," in almost every case, is both truth that diagnoses and mercy that delivers. Warning and judgment name injustice, idolatry, and honest need. Promise and grace announce "righteousness" that will "roll like a river" (Amos 5:24, AT), a day when "every knee shall bow" to the Lord (Isa. 45:23), and newness deeper than any need: a "new covenant" (Jer. 31:31), a new "heart of flesh" (Ezek. 36:26), and the word of the Lord who says, "Behold, I am doing a new thing" (Isa. 43:19).

Hope out of and after hopelessness also shapes the history. The book of Joshua opens on the edge of the land. The exodus generation

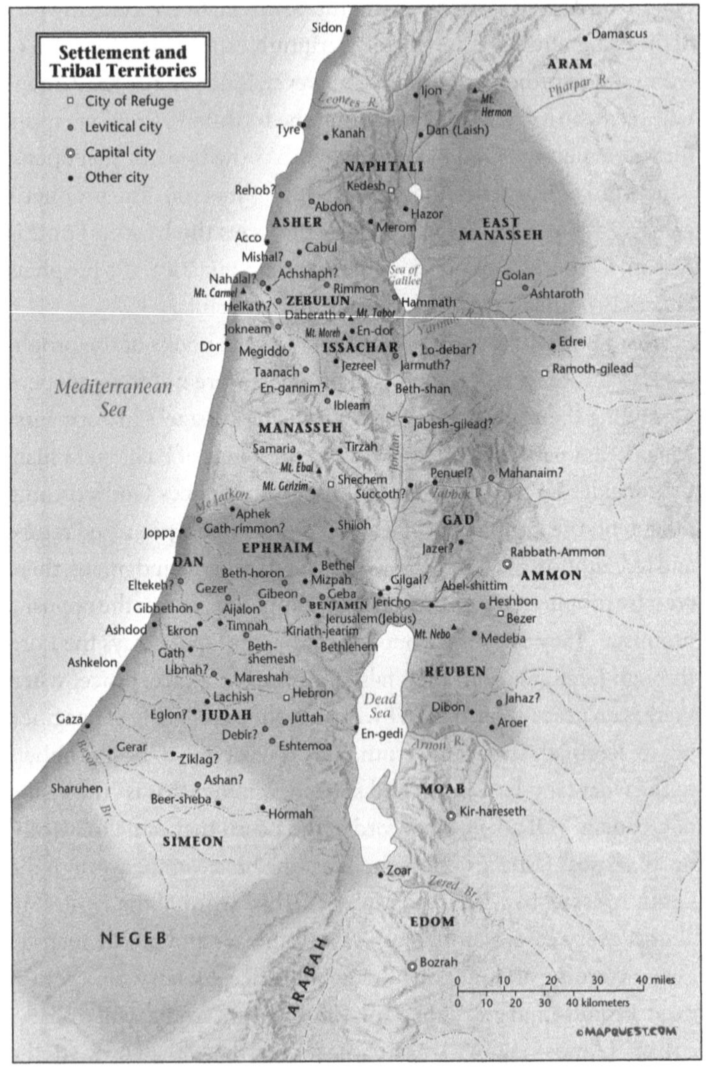

Map of Israel during Joshua's Time

has died, and the newly numbered people of Israel stand on a border: the banks of the Jordan are both a geographical divide and a fundamental question: Has disobedience and death disqualified us from and defeated God's promise? Or, in mercy and grace, will the waters part? The book begins on this border, but neither Israel's past nor the Jordan nor the inhabitants in the land are a match for God's mercy. The border is crossed; the longed-for land is now lived in; God and God's grace again are revealed to be stronger than fear, sin, and death. This promise, after a generation of wilderness and death, seems beyond the possible. But as another man named Joshua—*Yeshua,* or Jesus—once said, "With God all things are possible" (Matt. 19:26). Even the border of the "impossible," to quote Ernst Käsemann, "is not the boundary of hope"—when and where "that hope" is "in the promise of the God who raises the dead" (*Romans*).

The history of the prophets begins with Israel entering the land. The problem—and the pain—of the prophets is that this history ends with exile from the land. Moses had promised that the last of covenant curses—exile—would occur: "The LORD will bring you and your king . . . to a nation that neither you nor your fathers have known" (Deut. 28:36). This curse comes—to Israel in 722 BC and to Judah in 586 BC.

Israel's initial habitation in the land is not under the rule of a monarch. They are led by called and charismatic leaders referred to as judges (see the book of Judges). The people, however, desire a king like other nations, though the Lord warns Israel that their kings will exploit and enslave like other kings (1 Sam. 8). Saul, from the tribe of Benjamin, is Israel's first king (1 Sam. 9–10), but God's anointed is a descendant of Ruth and Boaz, a son of Jesse named David (see Ruth and 1 Sam. 16). David became the king of all Israel. The kingdom remained united under his son Solomon. But after Solomon's death, the kingdom was divided: to the north, Israel (sometimes called Ephraim after the dominant tribe), and to the south around Jerusalem, Judah. The refrain of the history of the divided kingdom, to take Amon as one representative, is: "He did what was evil in the sight of the LORD, as Manasseh his father had done. He walked in all the way in which his father walked and served the idols" (2 Kings 21:20–21). There are

Map of Israel and Judah

rare exceptions to this pattern: Hezekiah, who "removed the high places" of idol worship (2 Kings 18:4), and Josiah, who rereads and reaffirms "the Book of the Law" (2 Kings 22–23). The momentum of this history, however, is against the grain of the first commandment: from beginning to end, "the people of Israel did what was evil in the sight of the LORD and served the Baals" (Judg. 2:11), and Manasseh "did what was evil in the sight of the LORD" and "rebuilt the high places" and "erected altars for Baal and made an Asherah" (2 Kings 21:1–9). Israel's original sin at Mount Sinai is replayed and repeated, revealing again and again that the children of Abraham remain the sons and daughters of Adam.

And again, as Moses had warned, the final curse came. In 722 BC the Assyrians conquered and scattered the northern kingdom of Israel and Ephraim. Later, in 586 BC, King Nebuchadnezzar of Babylon laid siege to the city of Jerusalem, ultimately destroying both walls and temple before deporting many from Judah into exile in Babylon. Even in exile, however, the prophets seem to whisper, then speak, then shout and sing, "Even exile is not the end." That movement, from truth-telling judgment to beyond-curse blessing, shapes several of the prophetic books.

The word of the Lord comes to the various prophets at different times of Israel's history and as divine address to diverse circumstances. "The LORD raised up judges" before there were kings (Judg. 2:16), and the prophets declare, "Thus says the LORD," in the united, divided, destroyed, and exiled kingdoms. Micah, for instance, is a rural prophet who denounces the injustice and idolatry of Judah.

> Woe to those who devise wickedness . . .
>   because it is in the power of their hand. (Mic. 2:1)

> Hear, you heads of Jacob
>   and rulers of the house of Israel!
> Is it not for you to know justice?—
>   you who hate the good and love the evil. . . .
> who detest justice
>   and make crooked all that is straight. (3:1, 9)

In this context of oppression, misused power, and injustice, Micah proclaims "what is good" and "what the LORD requires of you: to do justice, and to love kindness, and to walk humbly before your God" (6:8, AT). Isaiah, by contrast, is an urban prophet, and his critique comes from an insider of the city.

> How the faithful city
> has become a whore. . . .
> They do not bring justice to the fatherless,
> and the widow's cause does not come to them.
> (Isa. 1:21–23)

Despite this diversity of time, context, and oracle, the prophets share a pattern. The Deuteronomic pattern, remember, is, obedience leads to blessing, disobedience leads to curse—and yet there is blessing even beyond the curse. The prophets announce this judgment and grace, and finally proclaim a mercy after and out of the curse: hope beyond exile, forgiveness stronger than sin, freedom from this new bondage, and life after and out of death. Not every prophet, in his specific context, imagines the possibility of human faithfulness and divine blessing. Nahum, for example, delivers "an oracle concerning Nineveh" (Nah. 1:1), a city that symbolized Assyrian corruption and power and to which Jonah had been called: "Arise, go to Nineveh, that great city, and call out against it" (Jon. 1:2). Nahum offers Nineveh no initial invitation to repentance and relief; his word is, "Woe to the bloody city" (Nah. 3:1), "the scatterer has come up against you" (2:1), "the Lord is avenging and wrathful" (1:2, AT), and "there is no easing your hurt" (3:19). The prophets experience and address the places and politics of their time. And still, again and again, the particular and "on point" words of the prophets follow a pattern: revealed and enacted diagnosis followed by promised and impossible deliverance.

Consider two of the longest of the prophetic books, Isaiah and Jeremiah. The dominant theme of the first thirty-nine chapters of "the vision of Isaiah . . . which he saw concerning Judah and Jerusalem" (Isa. 1:1) is judgment, woe, and warning. Even here there are hints: "to us a child is born" and "the LORD will have compassion on Jacob" (9:6; 14:1). But the headlines read: "the Lord GOD of hosts / is taking away from Jerusalem and from Judah" (3:1), "the Lord has sent a word against Jacob" (9:8), "Behold, the LORD will empty the earth and make it desolate" (24:1). In Isaiah 39, the final curse comes: "the days are coming, when all that is in your house, and that which your fathers have stored up till this day, shall be carried to Babylon. Nothing shall be left" (39:6). But here, in Babylon and beyond hope, a new word comes: "Comfort, comfort my people, says your God" (40:1).

> Fear not, for I am with you;
> do not be terrified, for I am your God. (41:10, AT)

It is the Lord who says, "Fear not, for I have redeemed you" (43:1), and there is hope even after exile because

> "I am the LORD your God,
> the Holy One of Israel, your savior" (43:3),

and "I am doing a new thing" (43:19). There will be restoration and redemption (49:8–26), and "every tongue will confess" that the Lord "is God and there is no other" (45:22–23, AT) because "the day of salvation" (49:8) will come with the Lord's "servant." This "man of sorrows" will be "wounded for our transgressions" and "crushed for our iniquities," and—mysteriously and mercifully—"with his stripes we are healed" (53:3–6). The God who called Israel out of Egypt promises an exodus from exile: blessing beyond the curse and grace beyond the grave.

"The word of the LORD" that is the prophetic "words of Jeremiah" (1:1, 4) begins when Jehoiakim is the king. During Jehoiakim's reign, Jeremiah's message is an exposé of unfaithfulness, an identification of "no peace" (6:14), and a warning that "disaster looms . . . and great destruction" (6:1). Later, when Zedekiah is king, this curse becomes concrete: "I will give Zedekiah king of Judah and his servants and the people in the city . . . into the hand of Nebuchadnezzar king of Babylon" (21:7). That this curse occurs is evident in Jeremiah 29:1, as Jeremiah writes letters to "all the people, whom Nebuchadnezzar had taken into exile from Jerusalem to Babylon." But again—and again and again—exile is not the end.

> "I have loved you with an everlasting love. . . .
> For the LORD has ransomed Jacob
> and has redeemed him from hands too strong for him. . . .
> I will turn their mourning into joy;
> I will comfort them, and give them gladness for sorrow." (31:3, 11–13)

Even "by the waters of Babylon" where Israel "sat down and wept" (Ps. 137:1), the Lord's "everlasting love" can sing a new "song" (Jer. 31:3, 12): "Behold, the days are coming . . . when I will make a new covenant with the house of Israel and the house of Judah." On this day, "declares the Lord: I will put my law within them, and I will write in on their hearts. And I will be their God, and they shall be my people. . . . For I will forgive their iniquity, and I will remember their sin no more" (31:31, 33–34).

Hosea and Ezekiel offer two further examples of this prophetic pattern of judgment and grace. Hosea was a prophet in the north to Israel; Ezekiel was a prophet in the south to Judah, who was taken into exile. These two prophets spoke at different times, in different contexts, and their prophecies take different forms. And yet, again, these two prophets share a pattern.

Hosea announces his prophecy principally by acting it out. "The word of the LORD that came to Hosea" (1:1) includes an embodied dramatic parable. God gives Hosea a message and calls the prophet to communicate it through a marriage. "Go, take to yourself a wife who is a prostitute," says the Lord, and Hosea "went and wed Gomer" (1:2–3, AT). And again, the Lord says to Hosea, "Go again, love a woman who is loved by another man and is an adulteress, even as the LORD loves the children of Israel, though they turn to other gods" (3:1). That last phrase captures the theme of this dramatic oracle. Israel is an unfaithful and adulterous bride, but even Israel's repeated unfaithfulness will be overcome by redemption. The whoring after other gods that is Israel's habitual and idolatrous prostitution brings Israel to a land of "no mercy" and a state of "not my people" (1:8–9). This judgment is enacted and uttered:

> Hear the word of the LORD, O children of Israel,
> because the LORD has a charge to bring against
> you who are living in this land. (4:1, AT)

But God's mercy promises a final marriage. "I will betroth you to me forever. I will betroth you to me in righteousness and in justice, in steadfast love and in mercy" (2:19). "No mercy" and "not my people" are not a last word.

> "And in that day . . . declares the LORD, . . .
> I will have mercy on No Mercy,
> and I will say to Not My People, 'You are my people.'" (2:21, 23)

God's "charge" runs from Hosea 4 to Hosea 13, and yet the Lord has loved and does "love" Israel (11:1), and promise and hope are the final horizon:

> I will heal their waywardness.
> I will love them freely,
> for my anger has turned away from them.
> I will be like the dew to Israel;

> he will blossom like a lily,
> he will take root like the cedars of Lebanon;
> his shoots will spread out;
> his splendor will be like an olive,
> and his fragrance Lebanon. (14:4–6, AT)

After the charge, despite the unfaithfulness, in the face of honest diagnosis, there is promise, mercy, deliverance, and finally life out of death.

Life out of death—resurrection—is the decisive image of "the word of the LORD [that] came to Ezekiel" (Ezek. 1:3). Ezekiel's prophecy unfolds as it finds Judah before exile and then follows Judah into exile. Ezekiel was among a wave of Jewish leaders taken as hostages to Babylon in 597 BC ahead of the destruction of and exile from Jerusalem that occurred in 586 BC. As judgment, siege, defeat, and exile are still on the horizon, Ezekiel's prophecy is warning and woe. This message takes the form of a model: "Take a brick . . . and engrave on it a city, even Jerusalem. And put siegeworks against it, and build a siege wall against it . . . and plant battering rams against it. . . . This is a sign" (4:1–3). Later this message is enacted as a prophetic march: "Son of man, prepare for yourself an exile's baggage, and go into exile by day in their sight. You shall go like an exile . . . for I have made you a sign for the house of Israel" (12:3–6). This pattern continues until this prophecy comes to pass. "In the ninth year, in the tenth month, on the tenth day . . . the word of the LORD" says, "Write down the name of this day, this very day. The king of Babylon has laid siege to Jerusalem" (24:1–2).

But again, in Babylon and beyond hope, "the word of the LORD" modulates from judgment to mercy. "I will restore the fortunes of Jacob and have mercy on the whole house of Israel" (39:25). There will be a new temple and a renewed city (Ezek. 40–48), and this redeemed people will be given a "new heart" (36:26). The temple and the city are destroyed, the people are scattered and exiled because of sin. The diagnosis Ezekiel offers is as deep as death. The question, to borrow from Walker Percy, is whether there is "love in the ruins," if God "loves you dead," and if there is hope even in the ruins because hope is in the God of resurrection (*Love in the Ruins*).

Ezekiel 37 asks this question *de profundis*—from the depths. The story is strange. "The hand of the LORD was on me, and he brought me out in the Spirit of the LORD and set me in the middle of a valley; it was full of bones. He led me back and forth among them, and I saw a great many bones on the floor of the valley, bones that were very dry. He asked me, 'Son of man, can these bones live?' I answered, 'O Lord GOD, you know'" (37:1–3, AT). The field was covered with bones, dry and dead, and then—there—the question comes: "Can these bones live?" This is the deep question posed by both the Pentateuch and the prophets. As Robert Jenson writes, this "is indeed *the* question. Does death win? Has it already won?" (*A Theology in Outline*). In Ezekiel, the answer is an announcement—a promise.

> "These bones are the whole house of Israel. Behold, they say, 'Our bones are dried up, and our hope is gone; we are cut off.' Therefore, prophesy and say to them, 'Thus says the Lord GOD: Behold I will open your graves and raise you from your graves, O my people. And I will bring you back into the land of Israel. Then you will know that I am the LORD, when I open your graves, and raise you from your graves, O my people. I will put my Spirit in you, and you will live, and I will settle you in your own land. Then you will know that I am the LORD; I have spoken, and I will do it, declares the LORD.'" (37:11–14, AT)

The diagnosis here is an honest description of human life and need: "our bones are dried up and our hope is gone." But a diagnosis even as final as exile and as deep as death gives way to the promise of deliverance that is both redemption and resurrection. The prophets declared both, and God's living and active word does both: it tells the truth that apart from Christ all are "dead in [their] trespasses and sins" (Eph. 2:1). This truth finds us in the tomb and seals it with a stone. But funerals and Good Friday are not God's final sermon. At the graveside—"among the ruins and the bones," to quote W. H. Auden (*The Sea and the Mirror*)—God says something that sounds like, "Little girl, get up!"(Mark 5:51) or "Lazarus, come out!" (John 11:43). It is a final sermon that rolls away the stone, and, in Ezekiel's words, opens your grave. This is the sound of "everlasting love" (Jer. 31:3), a love that nothing—not even disobedience or death—can separate us from (Rom. 8:38–39). This final sermon, this new song, has a name: Jesus Christ. He is the one who says, "I am . . . the living one. I died, and behold I am alive forevermore" (Rev. 1:17–18). As Paul sings,

> "O Death, where is your victory?
> O Grave, where is your sting?" (1 Cor. 15:55, AT)

Can these bones live? This is the prophets' final question. Their promise: "I will open your graves"—and behold, by grace, "He is not here, but has risen" (Luke 24:6).

CHAPTER 3

The Writings (Ketuvim)

THE THIRD SECTION of the Old Testament is the Ketuvim, or Writings. These writings include wisdom, history, and poetry ranging from Ruth to Daniel and Esther and Ezra to Psalms and Song of Songs. The history begins before and runs through the monarchy and united then divided kingdoms; much of the wisdom and poetry is associated with King David and his son Solomon, and some of the psalms are set in exile:

> By the waters of Babylon,
> there we sat down and wept. (Ps. 137:1)

The Writings, in other words, contain the memories and wisdom, the praise and prayers of Israel over the long and varied course of their history. This chapter will focus on the wisdom traditions and the psalms.

The wisdom literature of Israel contains two seemingly different traditions. Proverbs, to use the usual term, is pragmatic. Ecclesiastes and Job are speculative. Proverbs asks after and expresses the wisdom that runs with the grain of what God created and calls "good." Ecclesiastes and Job face a world and lives that seem far from good and allow confusion and pain to pose honest questions: Why is

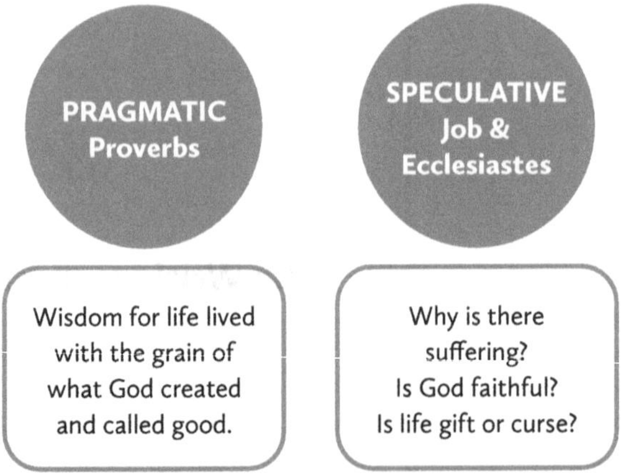

PRAGMATIC
Proverbs

Wisdom for life lived with the grain of what God created and called good.

SPECULATIVE
Job & Ecclesiastes

Why is there suffering?
Is God faithful?
Is life gift or curse?

Two Categories in Wisdom Literature

there suffering? Is God faithful? Is life a gift or a curse? Proverbs offers wisdom that takes place in the dust and drama of daily life by asking how: How shall we live? Ecclesiastes and Job speak from the dust and drama of a life that includes loss and ends in death and asks why: Why sorrow, why life, why death—God, why?

Proverbs reveals two fundamental characteristics of wisdom: wisdom comes from God, and wisdom is for life on the ground. In the New Testament, the letter of James describes "the wisdom from above" (James 3:17). Proverbs, similarly, refers to "wisdom" that is "received" (Prov. 1:2–3), and Wisdom herself—personified as the divine *Sophia,* or Wisdom of God—"cries out" to those who would "listen to" and "learn" wisdom (1:5, 20, 33). Wisdom is a gift from the Creator. This gift, however, is for the creature. The wisdom from heaven describes life on earth. God created and calls embodied and

Wisdom is the pattern of life, creaturely and communal, lived with the grain of what God created and calls good.

socially embedded existence good. Wisdom is the pattern of life, creaturely and communal, lived with the grain of what God created and calls good.

This wisdom that is from the Creator and for the creature is both heavenly and earthly: it is a gift from heaven; it is a gift for life on earth. Proverbs, in this sense, is practical—it engages the everyday, it imagines justice and peace in concrete relationships, and it offers "insight" and "equity" (Prov. 1:2–3; 4:1) for what Ecclesiastes calls life "under the sun" (Eccles. 1:9). This "from the Creator for the creature" framework raises two questions: What is the pattern of wisdom, and how is wisdom given and received? The former question is addressed in the opening and is the theme of the final two-thirds of Proverbs. The latter question, in part, is answered with a refrain: "Hear" (1:8), "receive" (2:1), "remember" (3:1).

Proverbs 1–9 is a repeated call to wisdom. Wisdom, according to Proverbs, is a gift Proverbs gives. To read—to hear, receive, and remember—Proverbs is to receive wisdom. "The proverbs of Solomon, son of David, king of Israel" are written to bestow and gift wisdom to the reader:

> To know wisdom and instruction,
>   to understand words of insight,
> to receive instruction in wise dealing,
>   in righteousness, justice, and equity. (1:1–3)

Wisdom "cries out" from the pages (1:20), and Proverbs keeps asking the reader to listen:

> Hear my son, your father's instruction,
>   and forsake not your mother's teaching. (1:8)

> Receive my words
>   and treasure up my commandments. (2:1)

> Do not forget my teaching. (3:1)
>
> I have taught you the way of wisdom . . .
> be attentive to my words. (4:11, 20)

According to Proverbs 3:19–20,

> The Lord by wisdom founded the earth;
> by understanding he established the heavens;
> by his knowledge the deeps broke open.

What Proverbs 4:11 calls "the way of wisdom" and "the paths of uprightness" is life with the grain of what God created good. But east of Eden and on the earth, life is out of line. Genesis 1–2 describe the creation God calls good, but Genesis 3 narrates a fall from the good that was to the life that now is. Sin and death describe life against the grain of created goodness, whereas wisdom is the pattern of life with the grain of what God calls good. This is why wisdom, and perhaps Proverbs in particular, is a two-edged truth. It describes what is good and with the grain of created life, but because it is given to those outside the garden, it exposes life lived against the grain. Wisdom, in other words, both describes and diagnoses. This double reality is often the experience of the reader. Proverbs identifies and pictures a just and wise pattern of relating to another person, for example, and the reader can sense the help and healing this wisdom offers. At the same time, however, the picture of Proverbs can be a mirror in which wisdom and life do not match. There is often—always—a gap between what is good and what is. Descriptions of wisdom, therefore, which offer needed and concrete guidance, can also become a diagnosis that produces the kind of wisdom that is both honest confession and a cry for deliverance.

The foundation and fundamental form of wisdom are given in Proverbs 1:7: "The fear of the Lord is the beginning of wisdom" (AT). This is a translation of the first commandment from law to life. "I am the LORD your God" and "you shall have no other gods before me" (Exod. 20:2–3) name a reality and call for an exclusive faith that is reflected and lived as "the fear of the LORD." What is and what is good is that God is God. The embodied and communal life that God calls good is created life—creaturely life. The Creator is distinct from the creature. "The fear of the LORD is the beginning" and the bedrock "of wisdom" because it confesses the Creator and lives as a creature.

This comes to dramatic expression in the book of Daniel as Shadrach, Meshach, and Abednego and then also Daniel say to the Babylonian king, "We will not serve your gods or worship the golden image" (Dan. 3:18) because they fear and trust only "the living God" (6:26), "the great and awesome" Lord "who brought [his] people out of the land of Egypt" (9:4, 15). Wisdom, in the face of forced idolatry, embodied "the fear of the LORD" as faithful worship of the one God who had delivered Israel from Egypt and who then delivers the youths and Daniel from the fire and the lions (3:8–30; 6:1–28). This wisdom of true worship did not mean exemption from the fire, but rather, as Johnny Cash sang, a "Fourth Man in the fire," a divine presence in, and only then deliverance out of, the flames. In the words of Isaiah, "Fear not, for I am with you" (Isa.43:5); "when you pass through the waters, I will be with you," and "when you walk through fire you shall not be burned" (43:2).

Created life—life with the grain of what is and what is good—is life by grace. From no need or necessity, out of no lack but from love, God in freedom and grace said, "Let there be . . ." Created existence is life as gift, and wisdom reflects and receives this as "good" and "very good" (Gen. 1:9, 31). Saint Augustine recognized the goodness and giftedness of the loved and yet limited life of creatures. "The fear of the LORD" that is "the beginning of wisdom" pictures two patterns of relationships. According to wisdom, creatures relate only to the Creator as the giver of life and source of salvation and joy. In relation to other creatures, wisdom recognizes that while a created gift or another creature can be both loved and good, it is

Wisdom: Life with the Grain of the Good

not God. Augustine's terms are *frui* and *uti*—a difference between "enjoying" the Creator and "using" or loving another as good but not God (*On Christian Teaching*). Much of the folly, however, of the finite and also fallen "fools [who] despise wisdom" (Prov. 1:7) is the confusion between Creator and creature reflected in the faith, hope, and love placed in goods that are not God. If "the fear of the LORD is the beginning of wisdom," the origin and expression of folly are fearing and having final faith in anything that is, however good, not God. As Martin Luther asked, "What does it mean to have a god?" His answer: "A god means that from which we are to expect all good and to which we take refuge in all distress. . . . That upon which you set your heart and put your trust is properly your god." Luther lists a number of common idols: "money and possessions," "skill, prudence, power, favor, friendship, and honor" (*Large Catechism*). David Zahl offers an updated and expanded list of what he calls "justifying stories" and "sin management systems." In his words, "career, parenting, technology, food, politics, romance," and more are often a "rebrand" of "the religious impulse," "that which we rely on . . . for meaning," "hope," and some final sense of being "enough" (*Seculosity*).

Ecclesiastes 2 offers a telling inversion of wisdom, a foolishness that expresses Luther's maxim that "the human being is . . . unable to want God to be God," but rather humans "want themselves to be god" (*Disputation against Scholastic Theology*). The "preacher" of Ecclesiastes, a "king in Jerusalem" (Eccles. 1:1), has attempted to be the Creator. "I made great works," and "I made myself gardens and parks" with "pools from which to water the forest of growing trees" (2:4–6). The "great works" of this would-be Creator expand to include animals and people: "male and female slaves" along with "herds and flocks" (2:7). The initial conclusion sounds like a good creation: "I became great and surpassed all who were before me in Jerusalem" (2:9). As the wisdom of Proverbs 14:12 reveals, however,

> There is a way that seems right to [people],
> but its end is the way of death.

In Ecclesiastes, the folly of this creation project of a creature is exposed. "I considered all that my hands had done and the toil I had expended in doing it, and behold, all was vanity and a striving after wind" (2:11). The preacher—Qoheleth (or Kohelet), he's called—runs through a list like Luther: toil, prudent living, wealth and honor, and the quest for wisdom (Eccles. 1–5). The verdict is always the same: "vanity of vanities . . . all is vanity" (1:2). The Hebrew word is *hevel,* and it unveils the folly and failure both of idolizing creatures and of self-creation. Final trust in all that is not God—including and perhaps especially oneself—is vanity and vapor, *hevel* or the unsubstantial and imaginary mists of idolatrous wishes that lack the weight of reality: God is God. It is "the fear of"—it is faith in—this one and only "Lord" that is "the beginning of wisdom." Created life is limited, but it lives from the love and grace of the Creator, who, through wisdom, invites dependent and finite creatures to the freedom of embodied and communal life that was created and is always good. The folly of faith in not-gods "is the way to death" (Prov. 14:12), but wisdom is "the fear of the LORD" and "in the path of righteousness is life" (12:28).

But life, Ecclesiastes says, always ends in death. "It is the same for all, since the same event happens to the righteous and the unrighteous . . . they go to the dead" (Eccles. 9:1–3, AT). The Greek tragedian Sophocles, even as he has a chorus celebrate "what a remarkable piece of work is man," cannot avoid a final limitation: "he cannot cure death" (*Antigone*). As demonstrated in the satirical, fake, but still factual headline from the *Onion*: "World Death Rate Holding Steady at 100 Percent." In W. H. Auden's words, "Where / the sun shines, brooks run, books are written, / There will also be this death" ("Nones," in *The Shield of Achilles*). The life Proverbs imagines, the life created good, appears to be gone. There is, at the end of life, a final question mark: death. This bedrock translates the question of wisdom from how to why. How is life wisely lived turns to why is life defined by loss and ended by death? The wisdom traditions of Israel in the Old Testament ask both questions. Together the depth and breadth of human experience are confronted, and it is especially Ecclesiastes and Job that face and voice the honest question—why?

In Ecclesiastes, "all [is] vanity and a striving after wind" is both the confession of a failed self-creator and the lament from "the living [who] know that they will die" (Eccles. 2:11; 9:5). There is freedom in the acknowledged failure, a return to the finite and receptive life of the creature who lives by grace. But if even this life ends in death, then perhaps all is vanity and vapor "under the sun" (1:9, 14; 2:11). There is "time for every matter" (3:1), "a time to be born, and a time to die," "a time to weep, and a time to laugh," "a time to love, and a time to hate" (3:2–8). This is all "time," however, life measured by moments that are always moving toward mortality: "after that they go to the dead" (9:3). "I saw vanity under the sun," says Qoheleth, and in this place of pain, tears, oppression, war, and death, "they had no one to comfort them" (4:7, 1; cf. 3:2–8). Hence one possible conclusion is "eat, drink, and be joyful" for, as Isaiah 22:13 remembers, "tomorrow we die" (Eccles. 2:24; 8:15).

This long look at life "under the sun" unearths the confusion, exhaustion, boredom, sorrow, and death that haunt human life. This kind of honesty, however, brings us to the end of our own resources and in that way "makes straight the way" of wisdom that is "the fear of the LORD" (Isa. 40:3; Prov. 1:7). To quote Auden again, "you will not find" the garden "until you have looked for it everywhere and found nowhere that is not a desert" (*For the Time Being*). Qoheleth looked for and even attempted to create this garden, but all was "vanity"—everywhere was "desert." There is, in the end and "under the sun," Auden continues, "the miracle." Sometimes it only comes after "all events have been studied" like they are in Ecclesiastes, but "miracle" and "life" arrive "when you have consented to / die" (*For the Time Being*). There, from the grave, "the vanity of human wishes" (Samuel Johnson) becomes the voice of final hope. There is freedom in this unveiled finitude, freedom to be real humans rather than imagined gods, creatures who receive rather than create and carry our life.

This gift of life and love, however, is not so much "under the sun" as it is from the Son who created all the stars (John 1:3; 1 Cor. 8:6). This king is, rather than pretends to be, the Creator, and he lived and died and rose "under the sun" and "for our sins" (1 Cor. 15:3). As creatures who are beloved children in the eternal Son, human life is freed to be human life. Rather than the endless and exhausting attempt to create dignity, security, significance, and what David Zahl calls "enoughness" (*Seculosity*), we are, as creatures and in Christ, gifted the value, peace, refuge, and verdict of "enough," which God gives to his forgiven and forever-loved sons and daughters. If death is the final question posed by life, the only answer is the death and risen life of Jesus Christ.

Suffering, loss, and life lived in the shadow of death are the setting and story of Job. "There was a man in the land of Uz who name was Job," and this man is identified as "blameless and upright" (Job 1:1, 8). Job "fears God," but the adversary ("the satan" or accuser) suspects this "beginning of wisdom" is only because of Job's blessings (1:9). Sorrow and grief, according to the adversary, always expose the human pattern: curse Job and he will curse God (1:11). Suffering on an almost incalculable scale follows: wealth and possessions gone, health turned to disease and pain, and sons and daughters dead. "He will curse you," the adversary suggested; "Curse God and die," says Job's wife in the face of these tragedies (2:9). Three others join the story, Job's friends who "sat with him on the ground seven days and seven nights, and no one spoke a word to him, for they saw his suffering was very great" (2:13). Their sympathy and silence, however, turn to accusation. The innocent prosper, and so Job must not fear God, proposes Eliphaz (Job 4–5; 15). Repentance is necessary because God punishes the wicked, insists Bildad (Job 8; 18). Job's pain and loss are less than he deserves, for the ungodly will always suffer, says Zophar (Job 11; 20). In Job's words, "Miserable comforters are you all" (16:2).

But is there any comfort? Is there anything to say or anyone who can speak in the face of real and deep suffering? As Job laments,

> "My spirit is broken; my days are extinct;
> the graveyard is ready for me." (17:1)

In the book of Job, it is not the adversary or Job or Job's wife or friends who speak the final word. After thirty-seven chapters of conversation, complaint, and condemnation comes the Creator. "Then the Lord answered Job out of the whirlwind" (38:1). This "answer," however, is a chorus of questions. "Where were you when I laid the foundation of the earth?" "Have you commanded the morning since your days began, / and caused the dawn to know its place?" "Have the gates of death been revealed to you?" (38:4, 12, 17). "Can you draw out Leviathan?" (41:1). Job's only answer is to say, "What shall I answer?" and "I will not answer" (40:4–5). As the Lord asks,

"Who then is he who can stand before me?
Who has first given to me, that I should repay him?"
(41:10–11)

The Lord's questions conclude and evoke a confession: "I know," says Job in the final chapter, "that you can do all things" (42:2).

The wisdom revealed at the end of Job rhymes with the wisdom given at the beginning of Proverbs: God is God. This is both the origin and bedrock of life and the final word on the far side of suffering and death. This God who is God, however, is also the one Job calls "my redeemer" (19:25). Even "at the last," says Job, "after my skin has been thus destroyed," "my Redeemer lives" and "in my flesh I shall see God" (19:25–26). This hope for redemption is hope for resurrection. The God who spoke to Job out of the whirlwind is also the God who, as Hebrews says, "has spoken to us by his Son" (Heb. 1:2). The God who "laid the foundation of the earth" and "shut in the sea with doors" and "has given birth to the frost" and "number[s] the clouds" (Job 38:4, 8, 29, 37) is also and finally the God "who did not spare but sent his own Son" (Rom. 8:32, AT). This redeemer does live (Job 19:25). As the angel declares in the Gospel according to Mark, "He has risen; he is not here" (Mark 16:6). Somehow, mysteriously and mercifully, "everything sad is going to come untrue" (J. R. R. Tolkien, *The Return of the King*). This does not mean there are no tears and that now is not "a time to weep" (Eccles. 3:4). Job and Ecclesiastes stare into the sun of suffering and death, asking the questions and not numbing the pain that plague life under the sun. This unblinking look at life under the sun, however, is also and finally a gaze toward the Son—"who loved me and gave himself for me"

"The fear of the Lord" is not so much a resolution to our questions as it is the faith in the God and Father of our Lord Jesus. This is the beginning and also the end of wisdom.

(Gal. 2:20). This redeemer lives. Christ is risen, and he "remembers my sorrows and bottles my tears" (Ps. 56:8, AT) and promises, "at the last" (Job 19:25), to "wipe away every tear from [every eye]" (Rev. 21:4).

The wisdom traditions of Israel in the Old Testament ask both how and why. The answer, in the end, is more like the questions directed to Job that reveal and remind us of the beginning and bedrock of wisdom: God is God. "The fear of the LORD" is not so much a resolution to our questions as it is the faith in the God and Father of our Lord Jesus. This is the beginning and also the end of wisdom.

—

Martin Luther once called Psalms "a little Bible." This collection of songs, he said, is a "fine, bright, pure mirror" in which "you will find yourself . . . as well as God and all creatures" (*Preface to the Psalter*). Saint Augustine, a thousand years earlier, used the same image: "Everything written here is a mirror for us" (*Enarrationes in Psalmos*). To read—to sing and to pray—the psalms is to behold a reflection: this is the range and reality of human experience and emotion; this is the God who speaks and hears, who promises and remembers. To read the psalms, however, is not only to see a reflection; it is to be in a relationship. The psalms are not only historical reports or ancient liturgical content; they are a medium and context of encounter. God

FIVE BOOKS

Psalms 1–41
Psalms 42–72
Psalms 73–89
Psalms 90–106
Psalms 107–150

PSALMS COLLECTIONS

Davidic: Pss. 3–41; 51–72; 138–145
Korahite: Pss. 42–49; 84–85; 87–88
Asaphite: Pss. 73–83
Songs of Ascent: Pss. 120–134

speaks through God's word, and yet the psalms are, at the same time, words given to speak to God. As Augustine writes, "If the Psalm prays, you pray; if it laments, you lament; if it exults, you rejoice; if it hopes, you hope; if it fears, you fear" (*Enarrationes in Psalmos*).

Psalms, or the Book of Praises, is a collection of songs. This collection comes from the breadth of Israel's history and reflects the full spectrum of Israel's experiences. This range of origin, situation, and emotion shapes the book of Psalms. The psalms are grouped together as five books and exhibit a variety of collections.

Each of the five books concludes with a benediction praising the Lord.

> Blessed be the LORD, the God of Israel,
> from everlasting to everlasting. (41:13)
>
> Blessed be the LORD, the God of Israel,
> who alone does wondrous things.
> Blessed be his glorious name forever;
> may the whole earth be filled with his glory.
> (72:18–19)
>
> Blessed be the LORD forever! (89:52)
>
> Blessed be the LORD, the God of Israel,
> from everlasting to everlasting! (106:48)

As the conclusions to these first four books suggest, the psalms are songs of praise. To quote the first and last line of the final psalm: "Praise the LORD!" (150:1, 6).

And the psalms do. The Lord is praised as the Creator (Pss. 8; 19; 65; 104), gratitude is given voice (Pss. 30; 34; 41; 66–67; 75; 92; 107; 116; 118; 124; 129; 136; 138), and the deliverance and promises of God are remembered as warning, hope, and worship (for example, Pss. 78; 89; 90). God is, in the words of Psalm 18:3, "worthy to be praised," both because God is and because this is the God of whom it can be said: "Great is his steadfast love toward us" (117:2), and "The LORD is my shepherd; I shall not want" (23:1).

This same psalm, however, sings from the shadows:

> Even though I walk through the valley of the shadow
> of death,
> I will fear no evil
> for you are with me. (23:4)

Many of the psalms are cries, as Psalm 130:1 says, "out of the depths." Lament is also the language of prayer.

> How long, O LORD? Will you forget me forever?
> How long will you hide your face from me?
> How long must I bear pain in my soul,
> and have sorrow in my heart all day long?
> (Ps. 13:1–2, AT)

Psalm 118, which refers to "the day that the LORD has made" (118:24), also remembers, "Out of my distress I called on the LORD" (118:5). In Psalm 118, this cry has already been heard:

> The LORD answered me and set me free. . . .
> The Lord is my strength and my song. (118:5, 14)

Sometimes, however, "the day the LORD has made" is still "the day of trouble," and the past and the promises turn to tears and questions:

> My soul refuses to be comforted. . . .
> Has his steadfast love ceased?
> Are his promises at an end for all time? (77:2, 8)

Luther's *Preface to the Psalter* captures the way the depth and breadth of Psalms give honest voice to the human heart.

> A human heart is like a ship on a wild sea, driven by the storm winds from the four corners of the world. Here it is struck with fear and worry about impending disaster; there comes grief and sadness because of present evil. Here breathes a breeze of hope and of anticipated happiness; there blows security and joy in present blessings. These storm winds teach us to speak with earnestness, to open the heart and pour out what lies at the bottom of it. He who is stuck in fear and need speaks of misfortune quite differently from him who floats on joy; and he who floats on joy speaks and sings of joy quite differently from him who is stuck in fear.

The psalms speak and sing from "the depths of the heart." This, for Luther, "is the greatest thing in the Psalter," both that it honestly pours out "from the heart" and that this honesty occurs "amid these storm winds of every kind." "Where does one find finer words of joy than in the psalms of praise and thanksgiving? There you look into the hearts of all the saints, as into fair and pleasant gardens, yes, as into heaven itself. . . . On the other hand, where do you find deeper, more sorrowful, more pitiful words of sadness than in the psalms of lamentation? There again you look into the hearts of all the saints, as into death, yes, as into hell itself." In all these songs and prayers and cries, the human heart is spoken to by God and also speaks "to God and with God." And here, before the God who, as Psalm 139:1 says, has "searched me and known me," the psalms pour "powerfully from the heart." The buried pain and hope and fear and joy are given voice, breaking the seals of secrecy and shame as "urgent" and honest words "burn and live" in prayer, lament, and praise to God (*Preface to the Psalter*).

Sometimes this sounds like longing and lament:

By the waters of Babylon,
there we sat down and wept. (Ps. 137:1)

Honesty, at other times, is confession:

Have mercy on me, O God,
according to your steadfast love;
according to your abundant mercy
blot out my transgressions. (51:1)

Pouring "from the heart," a psalmist can "give thanks to the LORD with all [his] heart" (9:1), remember that "unless the LORD builds the house, / those who build it labor in vain" (127:1), or recall that "the LORD has done great things" for us (126:3). Whether in Zion or Babylon, however, on "the day the LORD has made" or in "the day of trouble," both "beside still waters" and even in "the valley of the shadow of death," the psalms always sing of and pray to the one to whom Psalm 23 says,

You are with me;
your rod and your staff
they comfort me. (23:4)

This God is "a shield about me" (3:3), "our refuge and strength, / a very present help in trouble" (46:1). And this God who is "my shepherd" is finally the God who comes as "the good shepherd" (John 10:11), the one who walked "through the valley of the shadow of death" with the psalms on his lips: "My God, my God, why have you forsaken me" (Ps. 22:1; Matt. 27:46).

The psalms are, as Luther writes, for "everyone, in whatever situation they may be," because one can always find "in that situation psalms and words that fit the case." The psalms, however, are not only an honest pouring "from the heart," they are also "promises of Christ's death and resurrection" (*Preface to the Psalter*). "If the

Psalm prays, you pray," said Augustine. And the one to whom we pray is the one who has been with us in and has passed through "the valley of the shadow of death." To him, both now and forever and even "out of the depths":

> Praise the LORD!
> Sing to the LORD a new song. (Ps. 149:1)
>
> Let everything that has breath praise the LORD!
> Praise the LORD! (150:6)

PART 2

The New Testament

CHAPTER 4

The Gospels

THE GOSPEL OF JESUS CHRIST is a merciful surprise. This is the news of the New Testament. To hear the surprise, it is helpful to set the scene.

The end of the Old Testament is not the end of history. Israel was in exile under the Babylonians beginning in 586 BC, but return from exile was permitted under the Persians from 539 BC. Between the close of Malachi and the opening of Matthew, the Persian Empire was conquered by Alexander the Great. His Hellenic (or Greek) empire was divided after his death in 323 BC, and Israel moved from being under Ptolemaic rule to being under Seleucid rule, which gave way to the Maccabean Revolt and a kind of political autonomy under the Hasmoneans. When, in the Gospel according to Matthew, "Jesus was born in Bethlehem of Judea," the local ruler was "Herod the king" (Matt. 2:1). As the Gospel according to Luke records, this birth also occurred when "Caesar Augustus" ruled as the Roman *princeps*, or first Roman emperor. In 63 BC, Rome, under the generalship of Pompey Magnus, conquered Judea, and so the New Testament opens after half a millennium of exile and occupation.

Generations and generations of God's people lived in God's promised land, but the question is whether they were living fully under God's promised reign. There was a gap, an unrealized hope, between the presence of Roman power and God's promise. Jerusalem is the city of David, and yet descendants of David like Joseph and Jesus (see Luke 3:23–32; Rom. 1:3) lived under Augustus and, in the case of Jesus, died on a Roman cross by the order of a Roman official, Pontius Pilate, during the reign of the emperor Tiberius. Is this hope fulfilled? Is this promise come true? Is this, to borrow a phrase from the New Testament, God's "yes and amen" (2 Cor. 1:20)?

To open the New Testament is to encounter what Kavin Rowe calls "Christianity's surprise," news that, in the words of Acts 17:6, "turned the world upside down." Expectation and hope occasion confusion and misunderstanding: Who is Jesus? What has he come to do? Is he the awaited one? Is God now fulfilling the promises? Many of God's people longed for deliverance, a mighty act of God or a savior who would restore and redeem Israel. Under Roman rule, this hope for redemption often took the shape of military or political liberation: God would restore Israel by defeating the Romans. Jesus's conflict with Rome, however, ends not with Rome's destruction but with Jesus's death—death on a Roman cross. Jesus, according to the news the New Testament reports and proclaims, did not redeem Israel and make the world right by killing, but by dying. This "word of the cross," as the apostle Paul calls the message he announced, is "foolishness" and a "scandal" (1 Cor. 1:18, 23, AT). This shock, together with the gap between hope for a conquering messiah and Jesus as the crucified messiah, is both a repeated source of confusion and misunderstanding and also the deep spring of mercy, forgiveness, freedom, and life. From the Gospels to Revelation, the "word of the cross" is "scandal" and "folly," but it is also and finally, as Paul says, "the power of God for salvation" (1 Cor. 1:18–24; Rom. 1:16). As Jesus reads the prophet Isaiah in reference to himself: the Lord "has anointed me to proclaim good news to the poor . . . liberty to the captives . . . freedom to the oppressed," and "the year of the Lord's forgiveness" for all (Luke 4:18–19, AT). It is the news about this Jesus—the good news, "the gospel of Christ" (Gal. 1:7)—that turned the world upside down. This news was and always is surprise. This news is salvation.

Gospels & Acts	Letters of Paul	Other letters & Revelation
Matthew	Romans	Hebrews
	1 & 2 Corinthians	
Mark	Galatians	James
Luke	Ephesians	1 & 2 Peter
John	Philippians	1, 2 & 3 John
Acts	Colossians	Jude
	1 & 2 Thessalonians	Revelation
	1 & 2 Timothy	
	Philemon	
	Titus	

The New Testament is composed of twenty-seven different documents. Like the Old Testament, the New can be divided into three parts. First there are the four Gospels (and Acts). Then the thirteen letters of Paul (and the second half of Acts, which focuses on Paul's apostolic ministry). Finally, the remaining books, sometimes referred to as the General Letters and the Apocalypse, include Hebrews, 1–2 Peter, James, 1–3 John, Jude, and Revelation.

The New Testament opens with the four Gospels: Matthew, Mark, Luke, and John. This plurality is suggestive and significant. Does the fact that there are four gospel accounts mean that there is more than one gospel? Acts 4:12 insists that "there is salvation in no one else, for there is no other name under heaven given . . . by which we must be saved." As Peter says to Jesus in John 6:68, "Lord, to whom shall we go? You have the words of eternal life." There is, it seems, in the most fundamental sense, only one rather than four gospels. This one gospel is proclaimed by multiple witnesses. It was proclaimed earlier than it was ever written down by people who preached it. Peter proclaimed the gospel in Acts 2 in Jerusalem on the day of Pentecost. Paul proclaimed the gospel all around the Mediterranean world, mostly to gentiles, but also to Jews in and out of the synagogue. The letter to the Hebrews proclaims the one gospel. The Gospel according to Matthew is a written witness to the one gospel. In fact, the traditional titles of the four Gospels are not, for example, "the Gospel of Matthew" or "the Gospel of Mark." Rather, the names of these books are "the Gospel *according to* Mark," "the Gospel *according to* John," "the Gospel *according to* Luke," and "the Gospel *according to* Matthew." The gospel is and only is, as Paul says in Galatians 1:7, "the gospel of Christ." Each of the four Gospels, therefore, is the gospel of our Lord Jesus Christ according to Matthew, Mark, Luke, or John.

The oneness or singularity of the gospel was stressed and contended for in the earliest years of the church. Paul's letters record preachers whose messages the apostles identified as an "other gospel" that is "not the gospel" (see Gal. 1:6–10). The apostles identified and argued against these "not gospels" even as they clarified and declared "the gospel of Christ." To read Matthew, Mark, Luke, and John is to encounter that *one gospel* according to the witness that we call Matthew, Mark, Luke, or John. There are not, in this deepest sense, four Gospels in the New Testament. There is only one gospel of Jesus Christ, and every text in the New Testament, including the four texts called "the Gospels," proclaims this "power of God for salvation" (Rom. 1:16).

Another question is why these four texts are called "Gospels." Gospel is not an already-existing literary genre. The somewhat parallel biography-like genre in the ancient world was called *bioi* or lives: selective accounts of a historical person written to communicate something of the person's significance. And yet the Gospels are called Gospels: Why?

Mark was probably the first person to write down a gospel, and this evangelist also appears to be the first person to identify a written life as gospel, as an announcement of good news. Mark opens with the words, "the beginning of the gospel of Jesus Christ, the Son of God" (Mark 1:1). Before Mark used "gospel" to describe what he was writing, however, it was the word Christians used to describe what they were preaching. Paul traveled around the Mediterranean world and said he proclaimed the gospel (1 Cor. 15:1; Rom. 15:20). Paul did not write a text like the four Gospels; he declared a message he called the gospel. In Romans, Paul writes that this gospel both is "about God's Son" and is "God's power unto salvation" (Rom 1:1–4, 16–17, AT). When the earliest Christians said "gospel," they meant the news about Jesus that saves. The gospel is the story of Jesus that gives Jesus. The gospel is both remembered history and promised mercy. The gospel, in other words, is both news and grace: it proclaims and gives Jesus and thereby promises and gives freedom, forgiveness, peace, and life.

Another early reference to the gospel that the apostles preached is found in 1 Corinthians 15. Paul is reminding the church in Corinth of the gospel he proclaimed to them and summarizes that good news: "Christ died for our sins in accordance with the Scriptures, that he was buried, that he was raised on the third day in accordance with the Scriptures" (1 Cor. 15:3–4). That Jesus is Israel's messiah (the Christ), that what God has done in Jesus fulfills God's promises in Scripture, that Jesus's death was for our sins, and that death is defeated because Christ is risen: that, for Paul, is the good news. Each of the four New Testament Gospels preaches that gospel: Jesus Christ, crucified and risen for our redemption as the "yes and amen" to God's promises. (Interestingly, some other texts and traditions about Jesus from the ancient world do not proclaim this gospel, sometimes, for instance, disconnecting Jesus from Israel or suggesting Jesus was not fully human and so could not actually die. These documents or fragments are often called noncanonical or apocryphal gospels and are distinguished from the four canonical Gospels that all preach the one apostolic gospel; see Simon Gathercole, *The Gospel and the Gospels*.)

Back to the opening of Mark: "the beginning of the gospel of Jesus Christ, the Son of God" (Mark 1:1). Perhaps now it is possible to sense and see the significance of Mark calling what he wrote "the gospel." This is something more and different from an invitation to listen to good advice or even hear a true and significant story.

To write "the gospel" is to proclaim the story that brings salvation. By writing "the beginning of the gospel of Jesus Christ," Mark is communicating that this document is, fundamentally, a form of preaching the good news. Mark's written account is not simply a recording or remembrance of the life and death of Jesus. It is first and finally a form of proclaiming the life, death, and resurrection of Jesus that is the power of God unto salvation.

The four Gospels are preaching in the form of writing. That basic connection—the relationship between the one gospel and the four Gospels that narrate it—has significant implications for the hearing and reading of Matthew, Mark, Luke, and John. To open these gospels is to encounter the church's memory and history of the life, death, and resurrection of Jesus. But to encounter this history and memory as gospel is to hear the story of Jesus proclaimed as the power of God unto salvation. These writings are announcement and address: "Who do you say I am?" Jesus asked the disciples and also asks each reader of the Gospels (Mark 8:29, AT). Matthew, Mark, and Luke are, historically speaking, the best sources for knowing what Jesus said and did during his ministry. For the writers of the four Gospels, however, recording history is a form of proclaiming redemption. Matthew, Mark, Luke, and John are history and story as the news of deliverance and mercy. This is said explicitly at the end of the Gospel according to John: "these [things] are written so that you may believe that Jesus is the Christ, the Son of God, and that by believing you may have life in his name" (John 20:31). John wrote down the good news so that a person who reads or hears the good news might believe it and have life. All this meaning is present in the title of these texts: "the Gospel according to Mark," "the Gospel according to Matthew," "the Gospel according to Luke," or "the Gospel according to John." Each is a witness to the one gospel, the gospel of the Lord Jesus Christ.

This has implications for what we should be looking for when we read the Gospels. I borrow that phrase, "what to look for," when reading the Gospels from Martin Luther. In 1522, Luther wrote a short primer called *A Brief Instruction on What to Look for and Expect in the Gospels,* and it captures the singularity and substance of the good news:

> One should thus realize that there is only one gospel, but that it is described by many apostles. . . . Gospel is and should be nothing else than a discourse or story about Christ, just as happens among men when one writes a book about a king or a prince, telling what he did, said, and suffered in his day. Such a story can be told in various ways; one spins it out, and the other is brief. Thus the gospel is and should be nothing else than a chronicle, a story, a narrative about Christ, telling who he is, what he did, said, and suffered. For at its briefest, the gospel is a discourse about Christ, that he is the Son of God and became man for us, that he died and was raised, that he has been established as a Lord over all things. . . . There you have it. The gospel is a story about Christ, God's and David's Son, who died and was raised and is established as Lord. This is the gospel in a nutshell. Just as there is no more than one Christ, so there is and may be no more than one gospel.

This serves as a summary of the study of "gospel" thus far: there is one gospel, and it is the story of Jesus that is the power of God for salvation. Luther follows this observation with the question in his title: If the four Gospels are the good news of God's redeeming grace, what should a reader "look for and expect in the Gospels"?

> You should grasp Christ, his words, works, and sufferings, in a twofold manner. First as an example that is presented to you, which you should follow and imitate. As St. Peter says in 1 Peter 4, "Christ suffered for us, thereby leaving us an example." . . . However, this is the smallest part of the gospel, on the basis of which it cannot yet even be called gospel. . . . The chief article and foundation of the gospel is that before you take Christ as

> an example, you accept and recognize him as a gift, as a present that God has given you and that is your own. This means that when you see or hear of Christ doing or suffering something, you do not doubt that Christ himself, with his deeds and suffering, belongs to you . . . this is what it means to have a proper grasp of the gospel, that is, of the overwhelming goodness of God. . . . This is the great fire of the love of God for us, whereby the heart and conscience become happy, secure, and content.

Luther suggests a distinction (which he borrows from Augustine): the Gospels are not gospel because they offer a good example or provide good advice. The Gospels are first, fundamentally, finally gospel—good news. This means that to read the Gospels and encounter Jesus is to recognize that before he ever becomes an example for us, he is a *gift* given to us. Jesus is given in the gospel as a gift. As Luther says later, "The preaching of the gospel is nothing else than Christ coming to you," the promise that proclaims, "Christ is yours, presented to you as a gift." This is a clarifying and crucial distinction to remember when reading Matthew, Mark, Luke, and John. The actions, the words, the life, the death, and the life again of Jesus are not first an example to follow but a gift that is given. This gift is Jesus: the Son God "did not spare . . . but gave" (Rom 8:32), the "Son of God, who loved me and gave himself for me" (Gal. 2:20). The Gospels narrate and give the gift that is the one who lived and died and rose and reigns to redeem the world. As 1 Timothy 1:15 declares, "Christ Jesus came into the world to save sinners." To read the Gospels is to encounter Christ Jesus as he came into the world, living, dying, and rising as the grace that sets free, forgives, and gives life to those who are in bondage to sin and death.

Luther does return to the theme of example: Christ, first and finally received as gift, Luther says, will then "give your good works a good workout." To receive the gift of Jesus is to be redeemed, set free from having to establish, deliver, or validate ourselves, free from the bondage and burden of relating to God as if his valuing of and verdict on human life depended on human performance or pedigree. To "behold the lamb of God who takes way the sins of the world" is also to behold the God who beholds us, to see the God who sees us and says, in Jesus's name, "You are, already and always, my beloved child." It is this gift—what God has given to and done for us in Jesus—that frees us to go and "do likewise" (Luke 10:37). The grace of "neither do I condemn you" is a forgiveness that can free a person to "go and sin no more" (John 8:11, AT). To look at Jesus is to look on love, justice, wisdom, faithfulness, and compassion. His life is the "likewise" that recipients of the gift are called to "go and do." As 1 John 4:19 puts it, "We love"—we are freed to follow Jesus's example—"because [God] first loved us"—because Jesus is the gift given in the gospel.

But Luther is helpfully persistent about the priority and order. First and finally, the gospel is *not* about *what we can do for God* by looking at and living like Jesus. The gospel—and therefore the four Gospels—is about *what God has done for us* in the person of Jesus. What God has done for us is the story the Gospels tell: "the Word became flesh" (John 1:14), the Son of God was born the son of Mary and came "not to condemn the world, but in order that the world might be saved through him" (John 3:17). At the site of bondage, sin, and death, Jesus lived and died and lives again to bring freedom, righteousness, and life.

—

All of the Gospels—all of the New Testament, all of Holy Scripture—proclaim the gospel. This gospel, however, is not only general truth about God; it is news about Jesus of Nazareth that promises this single and specific Son of God "for our sins" (1 Cor. 15:3). In the gospel the past and living person of Jesus makes contact with personal pronouns: Jesus lived, died, and lives for you, for us, for me. This dynamic plays out in the New Testament as each document is both a perennial and a particular proclamation of the gospel. Paul's letters, for instance, always announce the "gospel of Christ" that is "the power of God for salvation," yet each letter was also addressed to specific communities as a pastoral intervention in the midst of real, concrete crises.

The way Matthew declares the gospel in his written gospel opens the possibility that this evangelist addressed a specific audience. There is, throughout the Gospel according to Matthew, a refrain: "this happened to fulfill what was written . . ." Jesus, Matthew emphasizes, is the fulfillment of God's plan for and promises to Israel. This is demonstrated and declared through a repeated identification of connections between events foretold by the prophets and events in Jesus's life. Matthew regularly names a prophecy and then indicates how Jesus fulfilled that promise ("this happened to fulfill what was written . . ."). Matthew opens before the birth of Jesus and continues all the way to and beyond the death of Jesus, showing that the birth, life, death, and resurrection of Jesus are the fulfillment of the plan, purpose, and promise that God made to Israel. Jesus is born in Bethlehem as "it is written by the prophet" (Matt. 2:5–6, quoting Mic. 5:2). Jesus's betrayal by Judas fulfills "what had been spoken by the prophet Jeremiah" (Matt. 27:9), and his cry from the cross, "My God, my God, why have your forsaken me?" is spoken with the words of Psalm 22 (Matt. 27:46). Again and again, as Matthew announces the good news, Jesus is the redeemer as the one who is, in Paul's words, the "yes and amen" to God's promises (2 Cor. 1:20).

This emphasis may suggest that Matthew had a primarily Jewish Christian audience. For any reader, however, these constant links to the history and Scriptures of Israel shape the way Matthew retells and proclaims the gospel of Jesus Christ. Matthew structures the narrative around five blocks of Jesus's teaching, recalling the five books of Psalms and the five books of Moses. Matthew also emphasizes the correspondence between Jesus's life and the history of Israel. For example, when Jesus was born, King Herod ordered the death of young boys in an attempt to eliminate the young would-be King Jesus. This parallels the action of Pharaoh

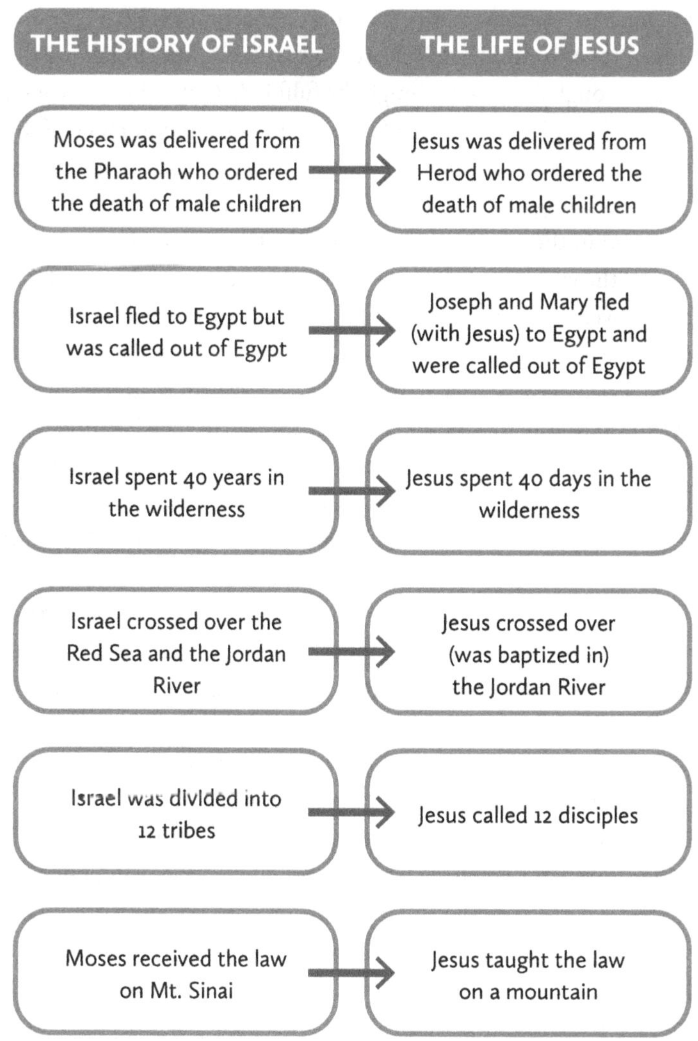

Parallels in Matthew

in Exodus, when Moses narrowly survives the Egyptian ruler's order to kill Hebrew sons. Jesus, as Matthew recounts, fled with his family to Egypt just as Abraham's children fled to Egypt during the famine. Matthew 2:15 makes this connection explicit: "[Jesus] stayed there until Herod's death, so that what was spoken by the Lord through the prophet might be fulfilled: 'Out of Egypt I called my Son'" (AT). Matthew reads this prophetic remembrance of the exodus also as a prophecy about Jesus. When Jesus came out of Egypt, echoing Israel's exodus from Egyptian enslavement, he was baptized in the Jordan River not unlike the people of Israel who passed through both the Red Sea and that same river Jordan. Jesus called twelve disciples to himself, reminiscent of the twelve tribes of Israel. Jesus spent forty days and forty nights in the wilderness, just as Israel spent forty years in the wilderness. And in Matthew 5, Jesus "went up on the mountain" to teach about the "law" (5:1; 17–18), recalling Moses's ascent of Mount Sinai to receive and then give the law. Again and again, Matthew remembers, recalls, and proclaims the life of Jesus in a way that stresses that Jesus is the fulfillment of God's plans, purposes, and promises to Israel.

Jesus's teaching in the Sermon on the Mount (Matt. 5–7) is world-upside-down wisdom. The poor and the persecuted and the peacemakers, the meek and the merciful and those who mourn, are the blessed (5:2–11). These are strange sayings, but Jesus does not speak as a scribe but "as one who had authority" (7:28–29). This, after all, is Emmanuel, God with us, and Jesus is interpreting his own divine law. His interpretation is intensifying and internalizing: "love your neighbor" comes to include "love your enemies" (5:43–44), and "you shall not murder" or "commit adultery" entails God's no to anger and lust (5:21–30). This is wisdom, life, and love from and for the whole human person, centered in the heart, and moving from the inside out, from who a person is (a good or bad tree) to why and then what a person does (motivation and good or bad fruit, 5:12–20). This is, as Paul says of the law, "holy and righteous and good" (Rom. 7:12). But one consequence of a "perfect . . . law of liberty," to use words from James (James 1:25), is that if the holiness, righteousness, and goodness, as Francis Spufford writes, are "not sized for human life: everyone fails" (*Unapologetic*). The

Sermon on the Mount is a picture of the life and love God not only imagines but promises to bring to pass.

But remember the poem from George Herbert: "look here; this is the thankfull glasse, / That mends the lookers eyes: this is the well / That washes what it shows" ("Holy Scripture I"). The Sermon on the Mount both shows the gap between perfect love and actual human life and washes it away. As Jesus announces in Matthew 5:17, "I have not come to abolish the Law and the Prophets; I have come to fulfill them" (AT). It is first and finally Jesus who lives and dies what the Sermon on the Mount says: Jesus "turned the other cheek" as Roman soldiers struck him (5:39), he "hungered and thirsted" in the wilderness and on the cross (5:6), he "mourned" and wept at the tomb of Lazarus and in the Garden of Gethsemane (5:4), and he is the one who "makes peace" through the blood of the cross (5:9). It is Jesus who "goes the extra mile" with the most degrading piece of shame, torture, and death on his back (5:41), and it is Jesus who "loves his enemies" and dies and prays for those who nailed him to that tree (5:43–44): "Father, forgive them" (Luke 23:34). Jesus, and only Jesus, is "perfect as" his "heavenly Father is perfect" (Matt. 5:48). And yet it is this Jesus who "came not to call the righteous, but sinners" (9:13), who says to all who are "weary and heavy-laden," "Come unto me and I will give you rest" (11:28, AT).

The Gospel according to Mark opens with an indication of what this story is and who it is about. This is "the gospel"—the saving news—about "Jesus Christ, the Son of God" (Mark 1:1). These titles identify Jesus as God's anointed and beloved king, the Messiah of Israel come to redeem all creation. For most of Mark, however, every time characters get close to naming Jesus, as at the beginning of this gospel, they are commanded to "be silent" (1:25). This is true of unclean spirits whom Jesus casts out and who know him as "the Holy One of God" (1:24) and a man with a leprous disease who is healed and told to "say nothing to anyone" (1:43), and even the disciples, after Peter confesses Jesus to be the Christ, are "charged . . . to tell no one about him" (8:29–30).

This secrecy seems to reflect the disconnect between expectations about a messiah and Jesus's mission as the Messiah. Under Roman rule and with a compromised and politically complicit religious leadership, many hoped for a messianic king or priest who would arrive as a military and political revolutionary, or perhaps as a religious reformer. This awaited and anointed one, many imagined, would mean the cleansing of the temple, the defeat of the Romans, and the reign of a new king on the throne in the City of David.

This gap between expectation and Jesus emerges most dramatically in Mark 8–10. Three times Jesus reveals the nature and purpose of his redeeming presence. Immediately after Peter confesses Jesus to be the Christ, Jesus "began to teach them that the Son of Man must suffer many things and be rejected by the elders and the chief priests and the scribes and be killed, and after three days rise again" (8:31). As Mark notes, "he said this plainly." And he says it two more times: in Mark 9:31 and Mark 10:33–34. Each time, however, they are unable to map these words onto their hopes about a messiah. After Jesus's first passion prediction, "Peter took him aside and began to rebuke him" (8:32). In the immediate aftermath of Jesus's transfiguration, in which Peter, James, and John heard the divine voice identify Jesus as "my beloved Son" (9:2–7), the disciples respond to Jesus's second passion prediction with an argument about which of them is the greatest (9:33–37). And finally, listening to the third and most detailed announcement of the betrayal, death, and resurrection that await Jesus in Jerusalem, James and John ask that when Jesus comes into his "glory," they be granted "to sit, one at your right and one at your left" (10:35–38). Moving toward Jerusalem with the one they believe to be the messiah, James and John expect victory, a coronation, a crown, and Jesus on a throne. Jesus's response, however, reveals again who he is and what he has come to do: "the Son of Man came not to be served but to serve, and to give his life as a ransom for many" (10:45).

As it happens, there is a coronation, Jesus does receive a crown, and he does take a throne. For the Romans who carried out this crucifixion the pomp and pageantry was mockery: "the soldiers . . . clothed him in a purple cloak, and twisting together a crown of thorns, . . . they began to salute him: 'Hail, King of the Jews'" (15:16–18). Following the pattern of a Roman triumph, Jesus parades through the streets before ascending a hill. This is not the Capitoline in Rome, however, but the place of the skull, Golgotha, and the march is not a celebration of violence and victory but a public display of defeat and death. But for all this irony, the inscription tells the truth: "The King of the Jews" (15:26). This king takes his throne, seated not on a fine chair inside a palace but outside the city hanging on the hard wood of a cross.

This is the surprise that turned the world upside down. Jesus, as his life and finally his death reveal, is the Christ, the Son of God, who reigns and redeems by suffering and serving. He told the disciples this "plainly" three times. Eating a final meal with them, he had taken bread and wine and said, "This is my body . . . this is my blood . . . which is poured out for many" (14:22–24). It is Jesus's death, however, that finally tears the curtain in the temple (15:38) and unveils the merciful heart of this Son of God. Out of the darkness and near death, Jesus cries from the cross, "My God, my God, why have you forsaken me?" He then "uttered a loud cry and breathed his last." As the Roman centurion overseeing Jesus's crucifixion "stood facing him" and "saw that in this way he breathed his last, he said, 'Truly this man was the Son of God!'" (15:33–39). Seeing Jesus die, this Roman soldier says who he really is: the Son of God.

"When the Sabbath was past, Mary Magdalene and Mary the mother of James and Salome" came to Jesus's tomb, only to find the stone rolled away and to hear the first Easter sermon: "You seek Jesus of Nazareth, who was crucified. He is risen; he is not here." Crucified and risen, Jesus is revealed as the Christ who reigns and redeems by suffering and serving. The charge to "be silent" now

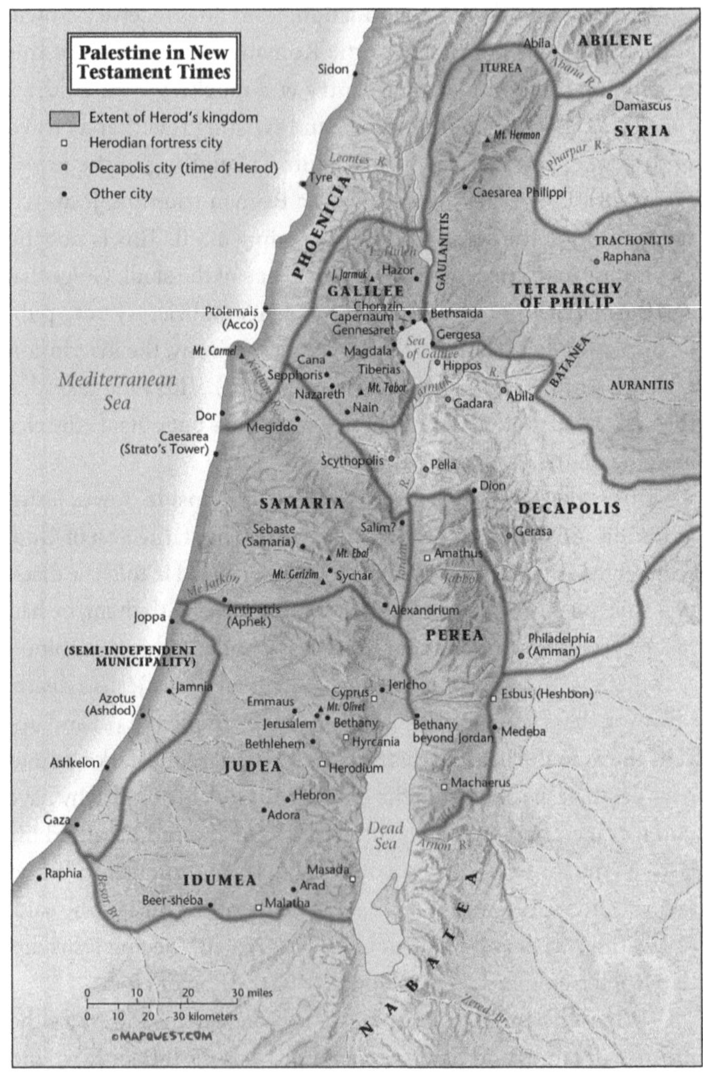

Map of Israel in the New Testament

gives way to "go, tell" (16:7), announce "the gospel of Jesus Christ, the Son of God" (1:1).

The Gospel according to Luke gives, as Luke says, an "orderly account" (Luke 1:3). This account begins before Jesus's birth and, together with Acts, traces the emergence and expansion of the early church. Luke and Acts are a two-part history. Both are addressed to Theophilus (Luke 1:3; Acts 1:1), and the ending of Luke and opening of Acts overlap. In Luke 24, the risen Jesus, just before ascending "into heaven," says to his disciples, "the Christ should suffer and on the third day rise from the dead" and "forgiveness of sins should be proclaimed in his name." The disciples are the "witnesses of these things," but they are instructed to "stay in the city until [they] are clothed with power from on high" (24:46–52). As Acts opens, the risen and about-to-be ascended Jesus addresses the disciples: "You will receive power when the Holy Spirit has come upon you, and you will be my witnesses in Jerusalem and in all Judea and Samaria, and to the end of the earth" (Acts 1:6–9).

Luke emphasizes two themes at the same time. There is an echo of Genesis in these emphases. Genesis 1–11 reveals God as the God of all creation whereas Genesis 12–50 focuses on God as the God of the covenant: the God of all is the God of Israel, of Abraham, Isaac, and Jacob. As the Gospel according to Luke and Acts proclaim the gospel, Jesus is the fulfillment of God's promises to Israel and, precisely in that way, the redeemer of the world. This theme emerges in the genealogy of Jesus, who is both a son of Abraham and a son of Adam (Luke 3:23–38). John the Baptist announces the salvation of "all flesh" (Luke 3:6), and Acts reveals Jesus as the one who "will rebuild the tent of David" and as the one upon whom the gentiles will call (Acts 15:16–18). The angels sing to the shepherds a song of "good news of great joy that will be for all the people" (Luke 2:10), and Simeon in the temple confesses Jesus as both "glory to [his] people Israel" and "a light for revelation to the Gentiles" (2:29–32).

This theme is also expressed in the overall structure and shape of Luke-Acts. The "orderly account" indicates a geographical pattern of narrowing and expanding: to Jerusalem, to only Jesus, and from Jerusalem, the gospel of Jesus to the ends of the earth.

Outside Jerusalem: Luke 3:1–9:50
Toward Jerusalem: Luke 9:51–19:27
In Jerusalem: Luke 19:28–24:52
Jesus: crucified and risen
In Jerusalem: Acts 1:1–8:1
Judea, Samaria, and Galilee: Acts 8:1–9:31
Toward the ends of the earth: Acts 10:1–28:31

In Luke, Jesus's ministry starts and stays in the north until, as Luke 9:51 says, Jesus "set his face to go to Jerusalem." Jesus then journeys south, and much of the material that is only in Luke appears in this section: the parable of the good Samaritan, for example, or the stories of those who search for and celebrate the return of what was lost, whether it be a sheep, a coin, or a son (Luke 10:25–37 and 15:1–32). These parables capture a Lukan motif: "Your [heavenly] Father is merciful" (6:36). This is the theme of Mary's song (1:46–55), and Jesus—"friend of tax collectors and sinners" (7:34)—and his parables portray a God of prodigal grace. Jesus arrives in Jerusalem with followers and the acclamation of the crowd, "Blessed is the King who comes in the name of the Lord!" (19:38). At the end, however, it is only Jesus: betrayed and abandoned by his disciples, outside the city, one moment, one man. All of God's promises gather together and come true on the cross. The Gospel according to Luke, and the story of all of Holy Scripture, narrow to this one place and this one person: Christ alone.

After his death and resurrection, however, the risen Jesus says in Acts, "you will receive power when the Holy Spirit has come upon you, and you will be my witnesses in Jerusalem and in all Judea [the region that Jerusalem was in] and Samaria [just north of Judea], and to the end of the earth" (Acts 1:8). Luke shows us God's plan and God's purpose, narrowing and narrowing until all is focused on the one place and the one purpose and the one person in whom God's promises come true: Christ alone, outside the city and crucified on Calvary. But once the promise is fulfilled, this narrowing gives way to expansion: "the word of God increased and prevailed" (Acts 6:7, AT; 12:24; 19:2). There is good news to proclaim—not just in Jerusalem, not just in Judea, not just in Samaria, but to the ends of the earth. This single Savior and this ever-widening circle of gospel proclamation is the structure of Luke and Acts: Christ alone and Christ for all.

Acts 2 opens with the fulfillment of Jesus's earlier "promise of the Father" (1:4). The apostles receive the Holy Spirit in Jerusalem, and on that day they preach the gospel to the crowd of "God-fearing Jews from every nation" who are in Jerusalem for Pentecost (2:1–5, AT): "this Jesus," who was "crucified and killed . . . , God raised him up," and "God has made him both Lord and Christ" (2:22–36). From Jerusalem, the circle of gospel proclamation widens. The disciples are persecuted and driven from Jerusalem, and as they scatter, the gospel spreads (Acts 8). As Acts 8:4 puts it, "Those who had been scattered preached the word wherever they went" (AT). Acts 9 relates Paul's calling, and Luke plays on his two names to capture the drama: "Saul was ravaging the church" (8:3), but after encountering the risen Lord, this same Saul is referred to by his Roman name, Paul, as he becomes the proclaimer of Jesus to the nations (an audience of the gospel confirmed by Peter's vision and experience of God's grace to the gentiles in Acts 10 and ratified by the apostles in Acts 15). This gospel is, as Luke-Acts proclaims it, "good news of great joy . . . for all the people" (Luke 2:10) because it announces Christ alone as redeemer of all.

Fourth and finally, the Gospel according to John. This witness to the one gospel of Jesus Christ is the most distinctive of the New Testament Gospels. Matthew, Mark, and Luke can be laid out side by side and compared because they have many of the same stories and sayings. For this reason, they are sometimes referred to as the Synoptic Gospels, meaning they can be studied or "seen together." In the Synoptic Gospels, there are often multiple accounts of a single event, for instance, the baptism of Jesus by John, Jesus feeding a crowd, a certain parable or healing. John, on the other hand, records stories and sayings the other gospels do not, like the wedding in Cana (John 2:1–11). And Jesus is active in Jerusalem earlier in his ministry in the Gospel according to John when compared to the more exclusively Galilean early ministry reported by Matthew, Mark, and Luke. Compared to Mark, where the action is fast-paced and Jesus's words are limited, John's narrative is comparatively sparse but Jesus's speaking and conversations are plentiful. In these and other ways, the Gospel according to John stands out. But perhaps the most notable distinctive, moving from Mark through Matthew and Luke and then to John, is that the Gospels keep moving the beginning of the story further and further back.

Mark, who is probably the first to write, opens with "the gospel of Jesus Christ, the Son of God." The next scene: "There was a man who came from God, his name was John" (John 1:6, AT). Mark begins his narrative with John the Baptist, right at the start of Jesus's public ministry. Matthew and Luke both open with an account of Jesus's birth, and both also include genealogies that place Jesus in the line of Abraham and David (and, in Luke's case, Adam). For the Gospel according to John, however, the beginning of the gospel is the beginning: "In the beginning was the Word, and the Word was with God, and the Word was God" (1:1). It is, announces John, "through" this Word that "all things were made" (1:3), and this one who "was in the beginning with God" is the "light" that "the darkness" can never "comprehend" or "overcome." And it is this Word, the Creator, who comes as a creature: "The Word became flesh and made his dwelling among us" (1:14, AT). This Word become flesh is "Jesus Christ," and "grace and truth came through" him (1:17). "No one has ever seen God; the only God, the Son who is at the Father's side, the one and only Son, the one who is from the Father, has made him known" (1:18, AT).

These first few verses make a startling confession and stand as a surprising invitation: Jesus was and was with God. This identification of Jesus as both the Son of God and one who is one with the one God is a refrain in the Gospel according to John. Jesus refers to himself as the temple, the place where the glory of God dwells, and eight times uses a form of the divine name to identify himself both with Israel and with Israel's Lord: I am:

The Bread of Life (6:35)
The Light of the World (8:12)
Before Abraham was (8:57–58)
The Door of the Sheep (10:7)
The Good Shepherd (10:11)
The resurrection and the life (11:25–26)
The way, the truth, and the life (14:6)
The True Vine (15:1)

This Lord, this Word, became flesh, and it is in his living and dying that God is fully and finally revealed. John 1:1–18 seems to say, to know who God is—the God no one has fully or finally seen—read this proclamation of Jesus's life, teaching, death, and resurrection. This suggests, after reading this gospel and beholding this "Lamb of God, who takes away the sin of the world" (1:29), the invitation is to see and say not only what Pontius Pilate said, "Behold the man" (19:5), but also: "Behold God." To the question, "Who is God?" the Gospel according to John replies, "Read this story."

This invitation to behold the glory of God in the person of Jesus is a sort of repeating climax throughout this gospel. John insists, again and again, not only that Jesus is the one who reveals God, but that he reveals God most fundamentally and finally at a particular

Matthew	Jesus is the fulfillment and embodiment of God's purpose and plan for Israel.
Mark	Jesus is the surprising king who reigns and rules by suffering and saving.
Luke	God's plan, enacted by one Israelite outside of Jerusalem, also includes Israel and the whole world.
John	Jesus is the one who reveals God, most fully and finally on the cross.

moment. One of the refrains for the Gospel according to John is Jesus's "hour." As he says to his mother, Mary, at the wedding at Cana, "My hour has not yet come" (2:4). In John 17:1, speaking to his Father, Jesus prays, "The hour has come." This "hour" is the time at which the Father will glorify his Son, that his Son may glorify him (17:1). Jesus has had this "glory" since "before the world began" (17:5), but he wants those he loves to see the glory the Father has given him because he loved him (17:24). There is an hour that unveils the glory of God, and this glory is revealed to be the love that is God (1 John 4:8) and God's love for the world (John 3:16).

John 12:27–33 indicates that this hour of "glory" occurs, as Jesus promises, "when I am lifted up from the earth" (12:32). As John comments, "He said this to show the kind of death he was going to die" (12:33). The light is dawning: the clear and climactic revelation of God in the life of Jesus is—mysteriously and mercifully—the death of Jesus.

My daughter, when she was about four, was reading Sally Lloyd-Jones's *Jesus Storybook Bible* at home with my wife. As they read, our daughter asked, "Mommy, what does God look like?" This, my wife understood, was her way of asking, "What is God like? Is God good? Can I trust God?" My wife could probably have found some kind of image. But instead, she did what the Gospel according to John—what all of Holy Scripture—does. She flipped to a different page and read my daughter a story that said:

> They walked up the hill outside the city. Jesus had never done anything wrong. But they were going to kill him the way criminals were killed. They nailed Jesus to the cross. "Father, forgive them," Jesus gasped. "They don't understand what they're doing." "You say you've come to rescue us!" people shouted. "But you can't even rescue yourself!" . . . But Jesus stayed. You see, they didn't understand. It wasn't the nails that kept Jesus there. It was love. "Papa?" Jesus cried, frantically searching the sky. "Papa? Where are you? Don't leave me!" And for the first

> time—and the last—when he spoke, nothing happened. Just a horrible, endless silence. God didn't answer. He turned away from his Boy. Tears rolled down Jesus' face. The face of the One who would wipe away every tear from every eye. Even though it was midday, a dreadful darkness covered the face of the world. The sun could not shine. The earth trembled and quaked. The great mountains shook. Rocks split in two. Until it seemed that the whole world would break. That creation would tear itself apart. . . . Then Jesus shouted out in a loud voice, "It is finished!" And it was. He had done it. Jesus had rescued the whole world. "Father!" Jesus cried. "I give you my life." And with a great sigh he let himself die.

My wife turned to my daughter and said, "That is what God looks like. And God did that for *you*."

That is a profound and pitch-perfect summation of the Gospel according to John: "In the beginning was the Word, and the Word was with God, and the Word was God." This "Word became flesh and dwelt among us," and though "no one has ever seen God; the only God, the Son from the Father's side has made him known." We behold this God as we "behold the Lamb of God who takes away the sins of the world." The "hour" of glorification happens outside of Jerusalem, on a hill called Golgotha. Jesus, crowned with thorns and mockingly but truly declared king, hangs enthroned on a cross: bleeding, dying, suffering because "God so loved the world."

John opens "in the beginning . . ." John ends with a new beginning. "On the first day of the week" and "while it was still dark" a woman looks for a man in a garden (20:1). This is a gravesite, and so a time of tears (20:11). But a new first day has dawned, and Mary Magdalene is addressed by the risen Jesus (20:16). The one who made the world became flesh to remake the world because "God so loved the world."

Each gospel preaches this one gospel: "Neither do I condemn you" (John 8:11); "The Son of Man came . . . to give his life as a ransom for many" (Mark 10:45); "Come unto me all you who are weary and heavy-laden and I will give you rest" (Matt. 11:28, AT); "I came to set the captives free" (Luke 4:18, AT). For now, John 3:16–17 can serve as the final sermon: "God so loved the world that he gave his only Son" who "came into the world not to condemn the world but so that the world through him might be saved" (AT).

CHAPTER 5

The Letters (and Life) of Paul

"WE PREACH CHRIST CRUCIFIED" (1 Cor. 1:23). This is a summary of Paul's only sermon: "I decided to know nothing among you expect Jesus Christ and him crucified" (1 Cor. 2:2). This "word of the cross," as Paul calls it (1:18), is "scandalous" and "foolish" (1:23, AT), but it is also and finally the "wisdom" and "power of God" that give "Jesus Christ whom God made our wisdom and our righteousness and holiness and redemption" (1:18, 23, 30, AT).

The scandal and merciful surprise of "the word of the cross" are captured by the collision between this message and "a mob" in Thessalonica: "these men" who proclaim the crucified and risen Jesus, the crowd charges, "have turned the world upside down" (Acts 17:2–6). Friedrich Nietzsche sensed that such a gospel entailed "a revaluation of all antique values" (*Beyond Good and Evil*). The cross is a site of weakness and shame, of degradation and death. According to "the word of the cross," however, "God was in Christ" contradicting and overcoming bondage, sin, and death with a mercy and love that creates freedom, forgiveness, and life (2 Cor. 5:17–21).

—

The New Testament sources for the surprise Paul received and then proclaimed are Acts and the letters of Paul. Part 3 is a more detailed

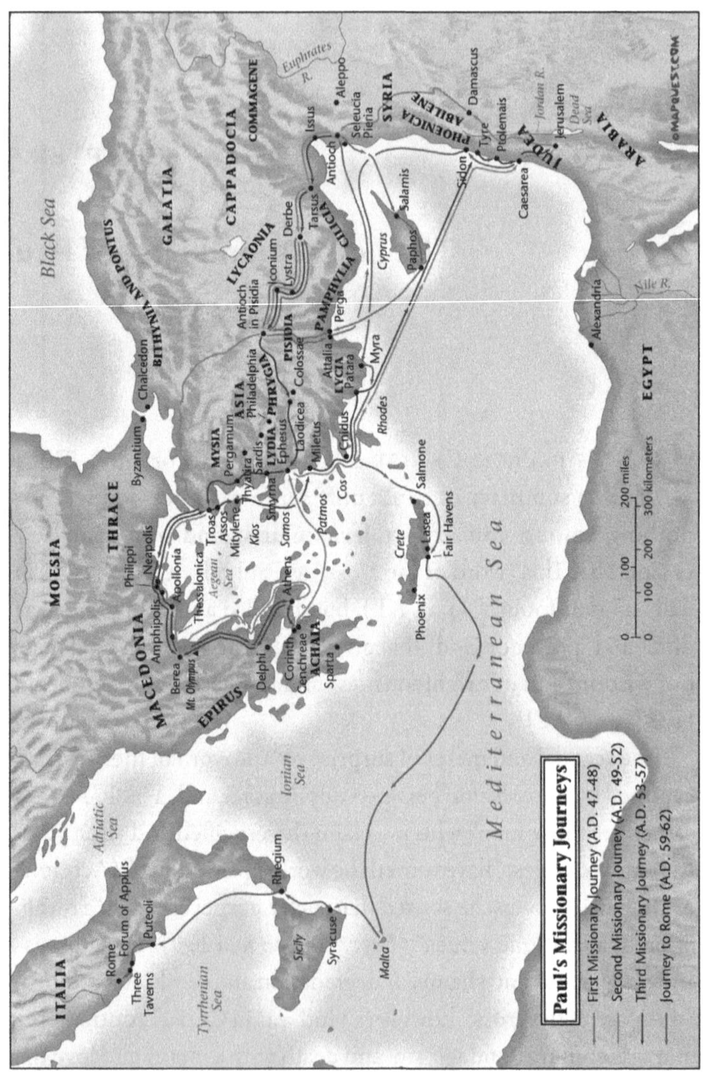

Map of Paul's World

study of one Pauline letter, Romans, which will explore in more depth the themes of righteousness and sin, Scripture and Israel, grace and boundary-crossing churches. This chapter is a general introduction.

Acts 9:1–19 narrates the surprise that came to Paul. "Still breathing threats . . . against the disciples of the Lord," Paul is traveling to Damascus when "a light" and "a voice" reveal the risen Jesus as "Lord" (9:1–5). This "calling in grace," as Paul calls it, is a "revelation of Jesus Christ" (Gal. 1:6, 12, 15) that finds Paul "unworthy to be called an apostle, because [he] persecuted the church of God," and yet, "by grace," calls him into being as a proclaimer of the merciful surprise that is "the power of God for salvation" (1 Cor. 15:8–10; Rom. 1:16). After this calling, Acts follows Paul's missionary journeys from Syrian Antioch around the urban centers of the Roman-ruled Mediterranean as Paul announces "the word of the cross" in Asia Minor, in Macedonia, in Greece, and finally, at the end of Acts, in Rome.

Reading Acts and the letters of Paul together, we see an apostolic and pastoral pattern emerging. Paul (and others such as Barnabas and Timothy) traveled to a city and proclaimed "the gospel . . . concerning [God's] Son" (Rom. 1:1–3) in and around the synagogues. As "the word of the cross" was often "a stumbling block to Jews" (1 Cor. 1:23), Paul moved to the markets or other meeting places to announce "the gospel" that "is the power of God for salvation to everyone" (Rom. 1:16)—Jew and gentile, Greek and barbarian, enslaved and free, female and male (Rom. 1:14–16; Gal. 3:28). Just as the "revelation of Jesus Christ" called Paul "by his grace" (Gal. 1:12–16), the "gospel of Christ" called into being, "by grace," communities Paul describes as churches or assemblies (Gal. 1:2–7). Once this still-small and vulnerable community was established, Paul continued his travels to repeat the pattern of proclamation. Paul's departure, however, does not mark the end of the pastoral relationship.

This is where the letters come in. After Paul left, the small and culturally strange churches experienced crises, confusion, and conflict of various kinds. Hearing the gospel of the one "who raised from the dead Jesus our Lord" (Rom. 4:24) entailed turning "to God from idols," thus posing a web of questions about the relationship between the church and the cults and culture of their context (1 Thess. 1:9). Paul proclaimed the defeat of death in the death and resurrection of Jesus, but a question mark is placed next to this promise by the continuing death of believers (1 Thess. 4:13–18). A gospel other than the one Paul preached came to Galatia after Paul, suggesting that faith in Israel's messiah required following Israel's law. The church in Corinth, it seems, experienced a vast array of confusion and conflict: from factionalism and immorality to denying the resurrection and questions about idolatry.

Paul's letters are pastoral interventions in the context of these crises. Despite his geographical absence, Paul letters are a form of pastoral presence. Sometimes Paul sent a coworker—Epaphroditus or Titus, for instance—to attend to and report on the needs of a community. The letters, however, are part of this ongoing pastoral care: written back to communities, addressing concrete sorrow, sin, and confusion by announcing again the word that both names honest need and, in the gospel, gives hope, peace, freedom, forgiveness, and life.

A few letters are partial exceptions to this pattern. Paul had not preached the gospel to those in Rome when he wrote a letter there (Rom. 1:15). The church in Colossae was called into being by the gospel through the preaching of Epaphras, so Paul's letter to the Colossians is also addressed to a community he did not establish. Epaphras, however, is among Paul's coworkers, and Colossians is therefore addressed to a community within the network of Paul's apostolic ministry. First and Second Timothy and Titus are addressed to individuals, as is Philemon, though the latter identifies a wider and more public audience: "Apphia," "Archippus," and "the church in [Philemon's] house" (Philem. 1–2).

To read the letters of Paul in the New Testament is, historically and literally, to read other people's mail. These letters are pastoral care and epistolary preaching to communities in the midst of suffering, doubt, conflict, loss, confusion, sin, and conflict. In this depth and range of crises, Paul declared "nothing . . . except Jesus Christ and him crucified" (1 Cor. 2:2). Paul's letters are contingent and concrete words of honesty and hope, but they are also and only "reminders" and reannouncements "of the gospel [he] preached to [the Corinthians]" (1 Cor. 15:1). Each crisis and question occasioned a renewed but never new proclamation of the one news that, in Oswald Bayer's words, "will never become old" ("Preaching the Word"). The exigencies of each context are a reminder that the gospel is always a particular and personal promise: it is "for us" (Gal. 1:4), "for me" (Gal. 2:20). The one promise, however, spoken at the site of concrete need, is only, always, and again the gospel Paul delivered to them: "that Christ died for our sins in accordance with the Scriptures, that he was buried, that he was raised on the third day" (1 Cor. 15:1–4).

That Paul wrote these words to Corinth is telling. The church in Corinth appears to have experienced an unprecedented range of doctrinal and ethical chaos and questions. There was sexual immorality and confusion about whether it was permissible to eat food that was sacrificed to idols (1 Cor. 5:1–13; 6:12–20; 8:1–13). The conflict between Christians was spilling out of the church into local courts, and some seem to have denied that believers would be raised from the dead (6:1–11; 15:12–58). These and other issues are part of and compounded by what Paul calls "divisions" and "quarreling" (1:10–11). Some, it is reported, are saying, "I follow Paul," or "I follow Apollos," or "I follow Cephas" (1:12). Paul's response is a series of questions. "Is Christ divided? Was Paul crucified for you?" (1:13). "What then is Apollos? What is Paul? Servants through whom you believed.... I planted, Apollos watered, but God gave the growth" (3:5–6). There is, Paul reminds the Corinthians, one gospel and one God. "There is one God, the Father, from whom are all things and for whom we exist, and one Lord, Jesus Christ, through whom are all things and through whom we exist" (8:6). This "one Lord" is "the source of your life in Christ Jesus, whom God made our wisdom and our righteousness and holiness and freedom" (1:30, AT).

It is not after but in the middle of this suffering and sin, these fractures and failures, that Paul writes of "righteousness and holiness."

The letter opens as an address: "To the church of God in Corinth, to those who are holy in Christ Jesus, called to be holy ones together with all those who in every place call upon the name of our Lord Jesus Christ. . . . Grace and peace to you" (1 Cor. 1:2–3, AT). Grace and peace and holiness are the first word, the foundation for, rather than the hoped-for outcome of, the letter. The church in Corinth, in the midst of chaos, confusion, suffering, and sin, are "holy in Christ Jesus." Not even schism or sin, it seems, can disqualify or disconnect those "in Christ Jesus" from the "grace and peace," the "righteousness and redemption," God gives through the gospel (1 Cor. 1:2–3, 30).

This pattern is evident in a bit of autobiography in 1 Corinthians 15:8–10. Paul "was unworthy to be an apostle, because [he] persecuted the church of God." "But," he adds as God contradicts and overcomes this unworthiness, "by the grace of God I am what I am." The Corinthians, by this same kind of surprising and creative grace, are righteous and redeemed in Christ Jesus. This "life" becomes the basis upon which the letter addresses the various issues in Corinth. Boasting, competition, comparison, and scorekeeping forget the upside-downness of "the word of the cross" that calls the weak, low, and foolish (1:18–31; chaps. 12–14). Division, idolatry, immorality, and doubt cut against the grain of what is real. There is "one Lord" in whom you are "loved" and have "life" and are "righteous" (1 Cor. 1:30; 8:6; 16:24). This is the first and final word: "grace to you and peace" and "the grace of the Lord Jesus be with you" (1:3; 16:23).

The crisis in Galatia occasioned a letter that identifies and argues against "another gospel" even as it defines and declares afresh "the gospel of Christ" (Gal. 1:6–7). The language, rhetoric, and emotion of the letter are intense, but they seem to be sourced in a foundational conviction that there is only one gospel that is actual good news for the bound and oppressed, the hurting and sinning, the weary and weak, the overburdened and the dead. Where the rest of Paul's letters offer gratitude in addition to the greetings, Galatians shouts, "I am astonished that you are so quickly deserting the one who called you in the grace of Christ and are turning to another gospel—not that there is another one" (1:6–7, AT). Paul continues: "But even if we or an angel from heaven, should preach a gospel other than the one we preach to you, let that person be accursed. As we have already said, now I say again, if anyone preaches a gospel to you other than the one you accepted, let that person be accursed" (1:8–9, AT).

A song by Josh Ritter translates this theme into a cry for help, riffing on and echoing Paul's phrase "let them be anathema." "Peter said to Paul" and then "Paul said to Peter," Ritter sings, and as the words become urgent, Peter's pain is given voice: "I got a girl in the war, Paul, I know that they can hear me yell / if they can't find a way to help her they can go to hell" ("Girl in the War"). At the site of honest need, "another gospel" cannot help, but "the gospel of Christ" adopts and sets free (Gal. 4:5–6), declares righteous and makes alive (2:16; 3:21).

Galatians maintains this intensity and pitch. "O foolish Galatians! Who has bewitched you?" (3:1). "Look: I, Paul, say to you that if you accept circumcision, Christ will be of no advantage to you. I testify again to every man who accepts circumcision that he is obligated to keep the whole law" (5:2–3). "I wish those who trouble you"—in this case insisting on the observance of the Jewish law that includes male circumcision—"would emasculate themselves!" (5:12, AT). "But far be it from me to boast except in the cross of our Lord Jesus Christ, by which the world has been crucified to me, and I to the world. For neither circumcision counts for anything, nor uncircumcision, but a new creation" (6:14–15).

As Paul interpreted the stakes, what was at issue in Galatia was "the truth of the gospel" (2:5, 14). This had been an issue before, in Jerusalem, where some demanded gentile law observance (2:1–10), and in Antioch, when Peter acted "out of line with the truth of the gospel," separating himself from gentiles and thereby "forcing gentiles to follow a Jewish manner of life" (2:14, AT).

In Galatia, it seems, some (probably Jewish Christian) preachers arrived with a gospel combining faith in Christ with observance of the Jewish law. For Paul, however, any gospel of "Jesus and" is not "the gospel of Christ." "I am astonished that you are so quickly deserting him who called you in the grace of Christ and are turning to a different gospel—not that there is another one, but there are some who trouble you and want to distort the gospel of Christ" (1:6–7). Galatians is an argument against this "different gospel" and an announcement of "the gospel of Christ." "A person is *not* righteous by works of law, *but* by faith in Jesus Christ" (2:16, AT). "Righteousness" is not "through the law" but is "the gift of God" through the death of Christ (2:21). Paul's antitheses, with their "not, but" grammar, identify and say no to the "different gospel" as they pick out and proclaim "the gospel of Christ." This "not, but" pattern of speech shapes proclamation: to speak the gospel, do not condition the gift of Christ by criteria of inheritance or achievement, but give Christ as a conditionless gift—grace for the suffering, sinful, captive, and dead that gives hope, righteousness, freedom, and life.

The addition of law observance to "the grace of God" that is "the Son of God" (2:20–21) does not complement or complete the gospel; it contradicts it. "Look: I, Paul, say to you that if you accept circumcision, Christ will be of no advantage to you. I testify again to every man who accepts circumcision that he is obligated to keep the whole law. You are severed from Christ, you who would be justified by the law; you have fallen away from grace" (5:2–4). According to Paul's apostolic arithmetic, the required addition of the law is the elimination of the gospel. The law, according to Paul, is "holy and righteous and good" (Rom. 7:12), but "a law was" not "given that could make alive" and "if righteousness is through the law, then Christ died for nothing" (Gal. 3:21; 2:21, AT). This entails a diagnosis of human need as deep as death and a gospel that gives life not through the law but only through the cross of Jesus Christ. For Paul, the gospel is not and never is "Jesus if" or "Jesus but" or "Jesus and." Even where the proposed addition is the holy, righteous, and good law of God, Paul says, "not by works of the law," but only and always through "the Son of God who loved me and gave himself for me" (2:16, 20). The gospel is, and only is, "the gospel of Christ" (1:7).

Gospel of Christ = Only Jesus Christ

Another Gospel = Jesus Christ and _____

To adapt a question from Dietrich Bonhoeffer, however, "Who is Jesus Christ for Paul?" (*Letters and Papers from Prison*). As Paul proclaims the gospel of Christ, Jesus is announced and confessed as "Lord" (1 Cor. 12:3), the son of David and "Son of God" (Rom. 1:3–4), the one "through whom are all things" (1 Cor. 8:6), and the one who is "our wisdom and righteousness and holiness and freedom" (1 Cor. 1:30, AT). "In Adam," Paul says, "all die," but "in Christ all shall be made alive" (1 Cor. 15:22; see Rom. 5:12–21). In the words of 2 Corinthians 5:14–21, "one has died for all, therefore all have died" and "in Christ" there is "new creation," "reconciliation," "the righteousness of God." According to Colossians, Jesus is "the image of the invisible God," the one by whom "all things were created" and in whom "all the fullness of God was pleased to dwell" (Col. 1:15–19). It is this divine Creator who dies as a creature, "making peace by the blood of the cross" and "reconciling to himself all things" (1:20). Divinity and deliverance are confessed in a single sentence: "God was in Christ, reconciling the world to himself, not counting their trespasses against them" (2 Cor. 5:18, AT).

Philippians 2:6–11 brings together many of the themes in an extended confession. Christ Jesus,

> who, because he was in the form of God, did not count equality with God a thing to be held on to, but emptied himself, taking the form of a servant, being born in the likeness of humankind. And being found in human form, he humbled himself by becoming obedient to the point of death, even death on a cross. Therefore God has highly exalted him and bestowed on him the name that is above every name, so that at the name of Jesus every knee should bow, in heaven and on earth and under the

> earth, and every tongue confess that Jesus Christ is Lord, to the glory of God the Father. (AT)

Jesus is identified both as being "in the form of God" and "taking the form of a servant." The one who is God by nature becomes a human being by grace. The one who creates life suffers death, even death on a cross. This one, as Isaiah announces, is the "Lord" at whose name "every knee shall bow" and "every tongue shall swear allegiance" (Isa. 45:23). But this Lord, whose name is above all names, is also, as in Isaiah 52–53, a suffering servant. Humbled to the point of death, even death on a cross, Jesus is "a man of sorrows" who "has borne our griefs," "was wounded for our transgressions," and "with his stripes we are healed" (53:3, 4–6).

"Christ died for our sins," Paul says in 1 Corinthians 15:3. This follows the one-for-others pattern of Isaiah's suffering servant (Isa. 52–53) and also the sacrificial imagery of Leviticus 16 and the Passover (Exod. 12). Jesus died in our place and for our sins as the "atoning sacrifice," as Romans 3:25 indicates in echo of Leviticus 16:13–15. The depth of human need, however, is not, according to Paul, exhausted by transgressions. Human beings who sin are also identified as "sinners" (Rom. 5:8) and as those who are "under sin" (3:9). The death of Jesus, as Paul proclaims it, is a mercy that meets and overcomes all aspects of this complex human condition. Sins are "covered," "not counted," and "forgiven" by the sacrificial and substitutionary death of Christ (4:6–8). "In Adam all die" and "condemnation" comes to all as "sinners" (1 Cor. 15:22; Rom. 5:13, 19), but Christ "died for all, therefore all have die. (2 Cor. 5:14) and "in Christ shall all be made alive" (1 Cor. 15:22). Sin and death are also powers that human beings are "under" (Rom. 3:9), enslaved to (6:20), and that can be said to rule or "reign" (5:14). The death and resurrection of Jesus Christ, according to Paul, is both "victory" over sin and death (1 Cor. 15:54–57) and deliverance of those who were under the "dominion" of sin (Rom. 6:14) and the "reign" of death (Rom. 5:14). "Jesus Christ," Paul confesses in Galatians, "gave himself for our sins to deliver us from the present evil age" (Gal. 1:4). It is this "gift" that demonstrates God's "love": "God demonstrated his love in that while we were still sinners Christ died for us" (Rom. 5:8, AT, 15–17). This grace and love is forgiveness (Rom. 4:7), redemption or freedom like the exodus (Rom. 3:24; Gal. 5:1), and death and life with Christ that is the end of the old "in Adam" and the "new creation" of those "reconciled in Christ" (2 Cor. 5:17–20). "Christ died for our sins," proclaims 1 Corinthians 15:3, and this event and news is "according to the scriptures": an atoning for us and instead of us like the day of atonement and the suffering servant, a representative as us and we in him like Adam in Eden, and an act of divine triumph and liberation like the exodus.

In Galatians 4:4–5, Paul writes, "When the fullness of time had come, God sent forth his Son"—the one who was and is "in the form of God" (Phil. 2:6)—"born of a woman, born under the law, to redeem those under the law, so we might receive adoption as sons and heirs" (AT). The Son of God became what we are so that, by grace, we might become what he is: beloved children of the heavenly Father. What Jesus is by nature, we are by grace: God's sons and daughters. Jesus is the Son who, in mercy and love, makes us sons. In Christ, God is the one to whom we cry, "Abba! Father!" (Gal. 4:7), and also the one who says to us what has always been spoken to the Son: "You are my beloved child, in you I am well pleased" (Mark 1:11, AT).

sins	**Sin**	**sinner**
Transgressions	Under the Power of Sin	Existence in Adam
Substitution & Sacrifice	Victory & Deliverance	Death & New Life in Christ
1 Cor. 15:3 & Rom. 3:24	Gal. 1:4 & Rom. 6:5–23	Rom. 5 & 2 Cor. 5:14–17
Isa. 52–53 & Lev. 16	Exod. 1–20	Gen. 3:1–24

The Death of Christ: Love and Grace That Is Sacrifice, Redemption, and Death and Resurrection

The "only Christ" and "by grace" pattern of Paul's theology also shapes the way he tells his own story. In Philippians, Paul opens with an apparent basis for boasting. "Though I myself have reason for confidence in the flesh also. If anyone else thinks he has reason for confidence in the flesh, I have more: circumcised on the eighth day, of the people of Israel, of the tribe of Benjamin, a Hebrew of Hebrews; as to the law, a Pharisee; as to zeal, a persecutor of the church; as to righteousness under the law, blameless" (Phil. 3:4–6). This record of inheritance and achievement reflects a distinguished pedigree and notable accomplishments. Such a résumé, as the last phrase suggests, seems like righteousness. Philippians 3:7, however, interrupts this boast with the word "but": "But whatever gain I had, I count as loss for the sake of Christ." In consequence of "Christ," all is "rubbish" and the only "righteousness" is not one's own but is "found in him" and comes "from God" (3:8–9).

The autobiography of Galatians has a similar shape.

> For I would have you know, brothers and sisters, that the gospel that was preached by me is not a human gospel. For I did not receive it from any person, nor was I taught it, but I received it through a revelation of Jesus Christ. For you have heard of my former life in Judaism, how I persecuted the church of God violently and tried to destroy it. And I was advancing in Judaism beyond many of my own age among my people, so extremely zealous was I for the traditions of my fathers. But when he who had set me apart before I was born, and who called me by his grace, was pleased to reveal his Son to me, in order that I might preach him among the gentiles. (Gal. 1:11–16, AT)

According to this retelling, at the start and with reference to his own past, pedigree, and performance, Paul is the subject of his own story: *I* was advancing. *I* was zealous. *I* persecuted the church. Then, however, the story is suddenly interrupted by the actions of another. "But when God . . ." *God* set me apart, *God* revealed his Son to me, *God* called me by grace. This call and grace did not come as a response to or reward for Paul's previous life. God is the one "who set me apart before I was born," says Paul, before Paul's life could be the rationale for God's gift. This, as Paul insists, is a calling in grace, an act of divine freedom and mercy whose only source is divine love. This grace did not come because Paul was worthy, nor is it withheld because he was unworthy—"I persecuted the church of God." This is a gift given not *because of* but *even though*: not because of Paul's pedigree or righteousness but even though Paul's past reveals him to be unrighteous.

That grammatical difference—the difference between God's giving and loving "because of" or "even though"—is the grammar of grace. This grammar and this grace is Paul's pattern of speech.

> Consider your calling, brothers and sisters: not many of you were wise according to worldly standards, not many were powerful, not many were of noble birth. But God chose what is foolish in the world to shame the wise; God chose what is weak in the world to shame the strong; God chose what is low and despised in the world, even things that are not, to bring to nothing things that are, so that no human being might boast in the presence of God. And because of him you are in Christ Jesus, who became to us wisdom from God, righteousness and sanctification and freedom, so that, as it is written, "Let the one who boasts, boast in the Lord. (1 Cor. 1:26–30, AT)

The grace announced in "the word of the cross" is upside down. It calls the not-wise and the weak, the not-noble and the nothing. This pattern, for Paul, is a promise, the shape of grace that proclaims the gospel as a merciful surprise: at the site of foolishness, sin, bondage, and death, God, "in Christ Jesus," creates "wisdom and righteousness," "freedom" and "life." Grace, not inheritance or history, defines and determines the deepest and truest reality. As Paul declares the new creation called into being by the gospel, Onesimus, who has escaped enslavement under Philemon, is to be received back as the person he is in Christ: "no longer as a slave but more than a slave, as a beloved brother" (Philem. 16). Referring to the Corinthians' past but then declaring their present, Paul writes, "Such were some of you. But you were washed, you were sanctified, you were justified in the name of the Lord Jesus Christ and by the Spirit of our God" (1 Cor. 6:11).

Ephesians 2 also reflects this incongruity of grace, the mismatch between God's mercy and those receive it. "In the place of two"—us and them—God's grace "creates one" by "breaking down the wall of hostility" and "making peace . . . through the cross" (Eph. 2:14–16, AT). This same grace, given to those who are "dead in the trespasses and sins" (2:1), opens the grave: "But God, being rich in mercy, because of the great love with which he loved us, even when we were dead in our trespasses, made us alive together with Christ—by grace you have been saved" (2:4–5). Grace is given at the grave; grace resurrects the dead:

> "Awake, O sleeper,
> and arise from the dead,
> and Christ will shine on you."
>
> (5:14; cf. 1 Cor. 15:54–57)

This pattern of grace as God's redeeming and resurrecting gift of Christ to the undeserving and dead runs through 1 Corinthians 15. Paul opens the chapter reminding the Corinthians of the gospel he preached to them (1 Cor. 15:1). "For I delivered to you as of first importance what I also received: that Christ died for our sins in accordance with the Scriptures, that he was buried, that he was raised on the third day in accordance with the Scriptures, and that he appeared to Cephas, then to the twelve. Then he appeared to more than five hundred brothers at one time, most of whom are still alive, though some have fallen asleep. Then he appeared to James, then to all the apostles" (15:3–7). Paul remembers and proclaims again the gospel of the crucified and risen Christ who died and rose "for our sins" and "in accordance with the Scriptures." At 1 Corinthians 15:8, however, his announcement turns to autobiography: "Last of all, as to one untimely born, he appeared also to me. For I am the least of the apostles, unworthy to be called an apostle, because I persecuted the church of God. But by the grace of God I am what I am, and his grace toward me was not in vain. On the contrary, I worked harder than any of them, though it was not I, but the grace of God that is with me. Whether then it was I or they, so we preach and so you believed" (15:8–11). This is the story of grace. On the basis of his own biography, Paul is "unworthy." And yet, and yet: "But, by the grace of God, I am."

The grace of God that is the crucified and risen Christ "for our sins" cuts the chains that bind our being loved to our biography. A human being is not, as Samuel Johnson feared, "fettered" to himself ("Know Thyself"); being enough is not based on a person's genealogical givens or social achievements. As the grammar of grace reveals in 1 Corinthians 15, Paul was unworthy, but by grace Paul is called. Was ______, but by grace am. That is the grammar of grace, and it shapes not only Paul's story but all stories. Israel was "under the law" "until . . . God sent forth his Son," and is now "redeemed" and "adopted" (Gal. 4:1–7). The Galatians, like those in Thessalonica or Philippi or Corinth, were "formerly . . . enslaved to those that by nature are not gods. But now" they are "known by God" (Gal. 4:8–9). "Not-wise" and "not-noble," but from nothing and by grace called wise, righteous, holy, and free "in Christ Jesus" (1 Cor. 1:26–30).

Being enough and being loved are not calculated as the sum of "what we have done and what we have left undone" (Book of Common Prayer). As Paul's antitheses about righteousness reveal (Gal. 2:16, 21; Rom. 3:28; Phil. 3:9), the value of and verdict on life is not based on a person's biography; it is grounded and given by God's grace: forgiven and free, righteous and loved. As some of the "trustworthy sayings" from 1 Timothy and Titus summarize this good news, "Christ Jesus came into the world to save sinners" (1 Tim. 1:15), and "he saved us, not because of works done by us in righteousness, but according to his own mercy" (Titus 3:5).

The question posed by the Pentateuch and prophets was: Are disobedience and death the end, or is there a "love . . . strong as death" (Song of Sol. 8:6)—a God and a grace stronger than death? The Paul who "knew nothing but Christ and him crucified" (1 Cor. 2:2, AT) is also the apostle who announces, "Christ is proclaimed as raised from the dead" (15:12). As Paul writes in Romans 5:8, "God shows his love for us in that while we were still sinners, Christ died for us." But this Christ who died "for our sins" (1 Cor. 15:3) is the one "God raised from the dead," and "together with him you who were dead in your trespasses" have been "made alive" through "forgiving" and resurrecting grace (Col. 2:12–14, AT). It is this merciful surprise that becomes Paul's song:

> "Death is swallowed up in victory.
> O death, where is your sting?
> O grave, where is you victory?" (1 Cor. 15:54–55, AT)

"God, being rich in mercy . . . loved us, even when we were dead." It is this mercy and this love that "made us alive together with Christ" (Eph. 2:4–5), and it is this "love of God in Christ Jesus" that Paul is "sure neither death nor life . . . nor anything else in all creation, will be able to separate us from" (Rom. 8:38–39).

CHAPTER 6

Hebrews to Revelation

"GOD IS LOVE," ANNOUNCES 1 JOHN 4:8. "IN this the love of God was made manifest among us, that God sent his only Son into the world, so that we might live through him" (1 John 4:9). This God, this love, this Son has been the subject of this study of Holy Scripture. The theme is less the human interpretation of Scripture than the address and action of God through Scripture. As 1 John 4:10 says, "In this is love, not that we have loved God but that he loved us and sent his Son to be the atoning sacrifice for us" (AT). The "living and active" word (Heb. 4:12) is the word of this God who loves, who is love.

The hope of this study of Holy Scripture has been to hear this living and loving word. As an analogy, the words of an art curator are not written as a replacement for viewing a painting or sculpture; they invite their reader to look, perhaps deeper and differently, but to come back to and encounter the art. This introduction to Holy Scripture is an invitation to read Holy Scripture—to return to and hear, hopefully more deeply—the word of the God who "so loved the world, that he gave his only Son" (John 3:16).

—

The final section of the New Testament runs from Hebrews to Revelation. This includes shorter epistles such 1–3 John, Jude, James,

1–2 Peter, and also the longer sermon-like and apocalyptic texts entitled Hebrews and Revelation. Hebrews and Revelation will be the focus of this chapter, but a few brief words should be said about the rest of these profound and powerful books.

The beautiful, moving, deep, and honest epistles of John, for example, were written in the context of conflict in a particular community. The community is beginning to split apart because some people are denying that Christ came in the flesh: "every spirit that confesses that Jesus Christ has come in the flesh is from God, and every spirit that does not confess Jesus is not from God" (1 John 4:2–3). The opening verses of the first letter of John are an intimate and passionate confession of who Christ really is. "That which was from the beginning, which we have heard, which we looked upon and have touched with our hands, concerning the word of life—the life was made manifest, and we have seen it, and testify to it and proclaim to you the eternal life, which was with the father and was made manifest to us" (1:1–2, AT). This Christ who came in the flesh, came to deal with sin. "If anyone says they have no sin, then the truth is not in them" (1:8, AT). This diagnosis unearths deep and honest need. "But if anyone does sin, they have an advocate with the Father, Jesus Christ the righteous. He is the atoning sacrifice not only for our sins but the sins of the whole world" (2:1, AT). First John understands that "our heart" often "condemns us," whether from the remorse of the past we cannot alter or the fear of a future we cannot control. But God's mercy unties the knots of the past and dispels the shadows of the future with forgiveness and a "love" that "casts out fear" (4:18). As 1 John 3:20 says, "whenever our heart condemns us, God is greater than our heart." First John also repeatedly calls its readers to "love one another" (4:12), insisting that "we love because [God] first loved us" (4:19). Love looks like Jesus, who "laid down his life" (3:16), and every "love one another" is an echo and effect of the "he first loved us": "In this the love of God was made manifest among us, that God sent his only Son" (4:9).

First Peter also proclaims that "Christ also suffered once for sins, the righteous for the unrighteous, that he might bring us to God" (1 Pet. 3:18). In the death of Christ, God the Son suffered for human unrighteousness and gave himself, who is "our righteousness" (1 Cor. 1:30). "By this joyful exchange with us," writes Martin Luther, the Son of God "took upon himself our sinful person and granted us his innocent and victorious person" (*Lectures on Galatians*). Peter, as an apostle, "announces to us the grace of God," says Luther. Peter preaches the "one gospel," the good news that "Christ took our place, rendered satisfaction for our sins, and destroyed them" (*Sermons on 1 Peter*). James reminds his audience—"the twelve tribes in the Dispersion" (James 1:1)—that wisdom is God's gift from above (3:15), but that this heavenly gift is active and embodied on earth, in the concrete care and love of visiting "orphans and widows in their affliction" (1:27). "Faith," according to James, is active in the world in the form of "good works" (2:14–26). The life and love of "doers of the word" (1:22) flow from receiving "the implanted word"—the powerful and merciful word of the gospel—"which is able to save . . . souls" (1:21). Jude writes at a moment of needing to "contend for the faith that was once for all delivered" (Jude 3) and encourages those who are "called, beloved in God" (1) to "keep [themselves] in the love of God" (21). This encouragement comes to those who are said to be "kept for Jesus Christ" (1) and in the confidence and worship of, as Jude concludes, "him who is able to keep [them] from stumbling and to present [them] blameless before the presence of his glory with great joy, to the only God, our savior, through Jesus Christ our Lord, be glory, majesty, dominion, and authority, before all time and now and forever. Amen" (Jude 24–25).

Historically, Hebrews is something of a mystery. Author, date, and audience are all hidden from view. From and to whom, where and when are all open and unanswered questions. The title, Hebrews, seems to be from the second century and is derived from the content: Moses and Melchizedek, sacrifice and priesthood. Hebrews itself reveals something of the prehistory of the community to whom it speaks. They "heard" the "message" that declares the "great salvation" (2:1–4) and have been instructed or catechized in the faith (6:1–2). In "the former days," these Christians "endured a hard struggle with sufferings" (10:32).

The pastoral need that occasioned the writing of Hebrews seems to be analogous to the "sufferings" of those "former days." Then, formerly, they were faithful. Now, at least some are "neglecting to meet together" (10:25), and there is pressure to "drift away" (2:1), of turning "away from the living God" (3:12), failing to attain the promised rest like Israel's wilderness generation (4:1, 11), and "growing weary and losing heart" (12:3, AT). In the words of the severest warnings, the current sufferings—whether they are inviting reintegration to Roman society or a return to Jewish law and sacrifice—are posing a fundamental question: Will you fall away (6:6) and "trample underfoot the Son of God" (10:29, AT)?

The message of Hebrews is a single sentence: "Jesus Christ is the same yesterday and today and forever" (13:8).

Hebrews is written at the site of an open wound. It comes with real warning. It also comes, finally, with real hope: the supremacy and singularity of Jesus Christ. The message of Hebrews is a single sentence: "Jesus Christ is the same yesterday and today and forever" (13:8). Who this Jesus is, confessed in the context of suffering and as the one and only comfort, is the theme of Hebrews.

"The Letter to the Hebrews" does not always sound like a letter. There is no from-apostle-to-audience greeting, as there is in the letters of Paul, Peter, and James. Whereas letters open and close with names and salutations, Hebrews starts and sounds like a sermon.

> In the past, at many times and in many ways, God spoke to our ancestors through the prophets. But in these last days, he has spoken to us by his Son, whom he appointed heir of all things, through whom also he created the world. The Son is the radiance

> of the glory of God and the exact imprint of his nature, sustaining all things by the word of his power. After making purification for sins, he sat down at the right hand of the Majesty in heaven, having become as much superior to the angels as the name he has inherited is more excellent than theirs. (Heb. 1:1–4, AT)

Hebrews begins with this expansive and jubilant confession of Jesus Christ. This is the Son by whom God has spoken, the one in whom God's glory and nature are revealed and the one through whom God's world is redeemed. This Son is the Creator and upholder of all and therefore the one who is above and before all. This eternal Son is also the one who became an earthly son:

> "You are my Son,
> today I have begotten you." (1:5)

The one who is the radiance and representation of the divine nature "became," in Athanasius's words, "what we are that we might become what he is" (*On the Incarnation*). The eternally begotten Son of God was "begotten" as the son of Mary so that others might become sons and daughters of God. This Son is superior to angels and Moses (Heb. 1; 3), is the great high priest and a priest after the order of Melchizedek (Heb. 4–5; 6:13–7:28), and is the final sacrifice and author and perfector of faith (8:1–10:21; 12:2). This song of the Son—the one who is before and above—is the constant hymn of Hebrews.

In announcing the finality and once-for-all sufficiency of Jesus's death for sin, Hebrews draws extensively on the images of temple and sacrifice. According to Hebrews 10:1–21, the cultic practices of atonement are promise and prefiguration: "the law has but a shadow of the good things to come" (10:1). As patterns and promise, however, such sacrifices required repetition: "every priest stands daily at his service, offering repeatedly the same sacrifices, which can never take away sins" (10:11). This points to and in the end gives way to the final and forever-forgiving sacrifice. "But when Christ had offered for all time a single sacrifice for sins, he sat down" (10:12). This "forgiveness" fulfills the promise of divine forgetting: "I will remember their sins . . . no more" (Heb. 10:17–18, quoting Jer. 31:34).

Jesus's posture makes this promise. In Hebrews 1 and 10, "after making purification for sins" and having "offered for all time a single sacrifice," Jesus "sat down" (1:3; 10:12). This sitting echoes and embodies Jesus's words from the cross in the Gospel according to John: "It is finished" (John 19:3). For us and for our salvation, there is nothing left to do that Jesus has not already done. Priests no longer need to stand up, and the blood of sacrifices no longer has to flow because sin has finally and forever been atoned for and defeated in the "for all time" death of Jesus. "He sat down." As Hebrews 10:18 concludes, "Where there is forgiveness . . . , there is no longer any offering for sin." In words from a prayer that echo Hebrews, "Jesus Christ," who "suffered death upon the cross . . . made there (by his one oblation, once offered) a full, perfect, and sufficient sacrifice, oblation, and satisfaction for the sins of the whole world" (Book of Common Prayer). There is, in relation to sin and salvation, nothing left to do that Jesus, the great high priest and final sacrifice, has not already done. "He sat down."

This confession of both the supremacy and the atoning finality of Jesus Christ is announced to sufferers as a word of comfort and hope. A detailed consideration of the shape and pattern of Hebrews brings out both the honesty and the hope. Throughout the book, Hebrews celebrates the superiority of Christ and the sufficiency of his sacrifice by declaring that Jesus is greater. Jesus is superior to angels (1:5–14; 2:5–9), to Moses and all the prophets (3:1–6). Jesus is the final high priest (4:14–5:10; 7:1–8:13). Jesus is the final sacrifice, the once-for-all offering for sin (9:11–10:18). The greater-than-ness and the once-for-all-ness of Jesus as Son and sacrifice is the refrain of Hebrews.

Structurally, Hebrews surrounds each of its words of judgment and warning with these exultations and declarations of the greatness of Jesus and the finished-ness of his redeeming mercy. Between the

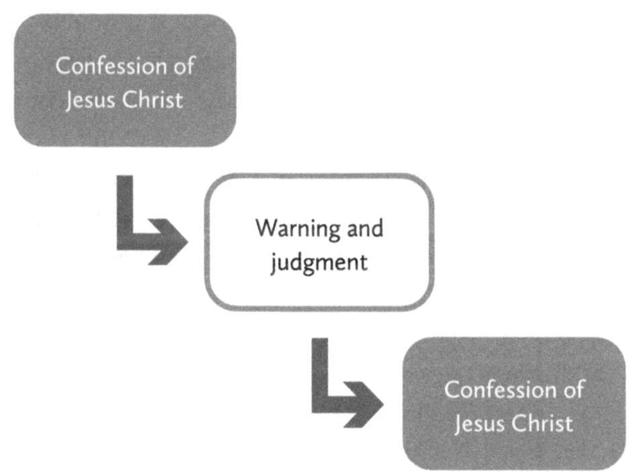

Pattern of Hebrews

celebration of Jesus as superior to angels and superior to Moses in Hebrews 1–3, there is a warning about not drifting away (2:1–4). Between the declaration that Jesus is superior to Moses (chapter 3) and that he is the great and final priest (chapters 4–5) comes a warning that recalls Israel's time in the wilderness when they grumbled and suffered from unbelief (3:7–4:13). Between the identification of Jesus as the great and final high priest (chapters 4–5) and Jesus as a priest after the order of Melchizedek (6:13–7:28) is the strong warning of 5:11–6:12. The warning of 10:22–36 is surrounded by the announcement of the new covenant and the once-for-all finality and sufficiency of Jesus's self-offering (8:1–10:21) and the review in Hebrews 11 of what 12:1 calls "so great a cloud of witnesses"—a series of figures who invite focus not on themselves but are occasions for us to "fix our eyes on Jesus, the founder and finisher of our faith" (12:2, AT). Again and in summary: structurally every warning is sandwiched between confessions of who Jesus is and what Jesus has done.

This structure and rhetorical pattern express the pastoral point. This study of Holy Scripture has encountered a recurring shape. "The word of God" that is "living and active," as Hebrews 4:12 has it, is "two-edged." God's word does two works, it is double and it moves in a direction: God unearths and names bondage, sin, and death in order to set free, forgive, and make alive. This is the twofold work of the living and active word of Hebrews: the warnings expose real and deep need for Jesus in order that the declarations of Christ that surround them can be songs and sermons that give Jesus.

The figure—and finger—of John the Baptist offers an analogy. "I must decrease and he must increase," John says (John 3:30, AT), and his preaching is a constant pointing to "the Lamb of God, who takes away the sin of the world" (John 1:29). Hebrews functions like John's finger. To read Hebrews is to hear warnings that unnerve and unsettle, that unveil what the novelist George Eliot calls "the futility of all other hopes" (*Janet's Repentance*). The strong and startling language of "crucifying again" and "tramping underfoot" (6:6; 10:29) evokes honest questions that expose the instability and shallowness of our own inheritances or achievements, the limitations and impotence of our pedigree and performance. If the question concerns the source of saving comfort and merciful assurance, any answer within the remit of our own resources is ash in this honest fire. But follow John's finger: wherever the reader runs in Hebrews, whether backward or forward from any warning, the one they run into is Jesus Christ—superior to angels and Moses and the greater high priest and final sacrifice who sat down. The structural enclosing of every warning between Christological confessions means the before and after of each unsettling is a sermon that sings of the gospel of Jesus Christ. Hebrews does what John the Baptist did, what Holy Scripture always does: it unveils need as it honestly diagnoses; it forgives and casts out fear as it preaches and points to Jesus Christ. "Behold," both the words and structure of Hebrews proclaim, "the Lamb of God, who takes away the sins of the world." The warning may expose "the futility of all other hopes," but there is, Eliot adds, one hope that holds: "his love alone" (*Janet's Repentance*).

An example will—I hope—make this pattern of unnerving and comfort more concrete. Hebrews 6 is perhaps the most uncom-

Isenheim Altarpiece (oil on panel, 1510–1515), Matthias Grünewald, Unterlinden Museum, Colmar, France

promising warning in the letter. "It is impossible to restore again to repentance those who have once been enlightened, who have tasted the heavenly gift, and have shared in the Holy Spirit, and have tasted the goodness of the word of God and the powers of the age to come, if they then fall away, since they are crucifying once again the Son of God to their own harm and holding him up to public disgrace" (Heb. 6:4–6, AT). Read in isolation, this warning might accomplish doubt and despair. A few verses later, however, Hebrews indicates that the horizon of this passage, however surprising, is hope. Even as "we speak in this way, yet in your case, beloved, we feel sure of better things—things that belong to salvation" (6:9). The end and aim of this warning is that those who hear it will "have the full assurance of hope" (6:11).

Surrounded by confessions that Jesus is the great high priest (Heb. 4–5; 6:13–7:28) and leading into the announcement of the once-for-all finality of Jesus's forgiving sacrifice (8:1–10:21), what the warning of Hebrews 6 does is cause the reader to recognize the futility of all hope "under the sun" (Eccles. 1:9). This raises a question like the disciples posed to Jesus, "Who then can be saved?" To which Jesus responds, "For human beings this is impossible" (Matt. 19:25–26, AT). Hebrews 6 urges, unsettles, and finally compels the reader to reach this honest and unnerving conclusion. For human beings, it is "impossible"—the word used both by Jesus and in Hebrews 6. But remember the rest of Jesus's reply to the disciples: "But with God all things are possible" (Matt. 19:26).

"Nothing can save us that is possible: / we who must die, demand a miracle," wrote W. H. Auden (*For the Time Being*). Hebrews both uncovers this impossibility and proclaims the miracle. The Son became "flesh and blood" so that "through death he might destroy the one who has power over death . . . and deliver all those who through fear of death were subject to lifelong slavery" (Heb. 2:14–15). Hebrews loosens the reader's grip on "all other hopes," but in that way it proclaims and points to Jesus in whose loving grasp they are securely and forever held. According to this pastoral pattern, Hebrews evokes the honest cry—"Who will deliver me?" (Rom. 7:24)—and then, finally and loudly, it repeats its hymn: "Thanks be to God through Jesus Christ our Lord!" (Rom. 7:25)—the one who is greater than angels and Moses, the seated high priest and once-for-all sacrifice. Hebrews is the finger of John the Baptist, always and ever preaching a single sermon: "Fix your eyes on Jesus, the founder and finisher of our faith" (Heb. 12:2, AT); whatever you may experience today or tomorrow, "Jesus Christ is the same yesterday and today and forever" (13:8).

At the end of the New Testament is a book that many think is all about the end: the last book, Revelation, is about the last things (*eschata*, in Greek). Revelation does promise an end—life with God—and prophecy is among its genres: "the words of this prophecy" are given by God "to show to his servants the things that must soon take place" (Rev. 1:3, 1). To begin to understand

Revelation, however, it is helpful to ask what "revelation" means. Although the style and imagery of Revelation can seem strange and different (both in general and compared to other parts of the New Testament), this genre of literature was widespread, especially among Jewish authors. As a type of text, Revelation—or at least most of it—can be classified as apocalyptic literature. There are many examples of this genre, some even included in parts of the Old Testament prophets. The book of Daniel, for instance, uses apocalyptic images and idioms. "In my vision at night, I looked, and there before me were the four winds of heaven churning up the great sea. Four great beasts, each different from the others, came up out of the sea. The first was like a lion, and it had the wings of an eagle. I watched until its wings were torn off" (Dan. 7:2–4, AT). There are also other Jewish texts that are not in the Old Testament, for example, 1 Enoch and 4 Ezra, that promise a thousand-year reign of a messianic figure or use language like Daniel's to describe a coming redeemer or ruler. "For my son, the messiah shall be revealed with those that are with him, and they that remain shall rejoice within four hundred years. . . . And the world shall be turned into the old silence seven days, like as in the former judgments. . . . And the earth shall restore those that are asleep in her, and so shall the dust those that dwell in silence. . . . And the most High shall appear upon the seat of judgment, and misery shall pass away, and the long suffering shall have an end" (4 Ezra 7). There is a sound, a scenery, a seeing in these texts that bears a family resemblance to Revelation. Consider, also, Mark 13, when Jesus spoke about the destruction of Jerusalem and the coming judgment, or Matthew 27, as the sun stops shining and graves open as Jesus is crucified. This language and imagery might still sound strange, but apocalyptic is not alien to the first-century world.

"The revelation of Jesus Christ" (Rev. 1:1). These are the opening words of Revelation, and they sound the theme: Revelation shows Jesus Christ. The word "revelation" translates a Greek word that means unveiling, a showing of what is but is unseen. The word suggests a veil that is blocking a viewer from beholding what is real. An apocalypse, or a revelation, is an event or an experience that lifts up that curtain so that there is sight. It is as if the reader of Revelation is in a theater when the show is about to start. The stage is ready. The actors are behind the curtain, and the action is about to begin. This side of the curtain, the reality on stage is veiled. But then the curtain goes up and: behold.

Revelation is not a riddle but reality, the unveiling that invites the reader to see, enter, and experience what is real.

With all the fantastical images and language of apocalyptic literature, with all its symbolism and drama, the claim of Revelation is that what it shows is fundamentally what is real. As the poet W. H. Auden once wrote, "What is real is what will strike you as really absurd" (*For the Time Being*). In apocalyptic literature, the curtain goes up, and what is finally seen is what is real. In that way, Revelation is not a riddle but reality, the unveiling that invites the reader to see, enter, and experience what is real.

Revelation, however, does more than declare and enact a dramatic unveiling. In unveiling the real, Revelation unveils a specific something, a specific someone. It is, as the opening words announce, a revelation and unveiling of Jesus Christ. The many images and the surprising and strange symbols of Revelation can feel like an overwhelming cascade. But according to Revelation 1:1, this flood has a focus: this is the revelation of Jesus Christ. He is, as Revelation reveals, "the faithful witness, the firstborn of the dead, and the ruler of kings on earth." Jesus is the "the one who loves us and has freed us from our sins by his blood," the "Alpha and the Omega" who "is and who was and who is to come, the Almighty" (1:5–8).

Revelation, as a whole and most fundamentally, is an unveiling, an apocalypse. This revelation of Jesus Christ, however, also contains seven letters addressed to seven different churches, each of which reflects a distinct situation. The church in Ephesus, for example, has displayed "patient endurance" but has also "abandoned the love [they] had at first" (2:2–4). The churches in Smyrna and Pergamum had experienced intense (and in at least one case, even fatal) suffering (2:8–17). In Laodicea, the church is described as tepid, neither hot nor cold (3:15–22). These different churches and these distinct contexts all receive the same revelation. The living and active word encounters and accomplishes God's purposes: to some, perhaps the faithless or the lukewarm, it convicts; to the suffering and oppressed, it comforts. The several churches require and receive the one revelation. Despite the *multiplicity* of audiences and situations, what the seven churches—what all churches, always—most need to hear and see is the *singular* revelation of Jesus Christ.

One more brief introductory issue: while John the Seer is the scribe of Revelation, the text is not John's but Jesus's revelation. John is instructed to look and write what he saw (1:19), but he is a witness, the scribe but not the source or the subject of this revelation. Revelation itself belongs to the revealer and the one who is revealed, Jesus Christ. Jesus is the one who reveals; Jesus is the one who is revealed. Seeing "the Almighty," John falls in fear. But the "Alpha and the Omega" speaks, "Fear not, I am the first and the last, and the living one. I died, and behold I am alive forevermore" (1:17–18).

When the curtain goes up, when the veil is lifted, reality is revealed: God is God. God is on the throne. God is being worshiped. In Revelation 4, the vision opens with the divine throne, where four living creatures unceasingly proclaim, "Holy, holy, holy, is the Lord God Almighty" (4:8). What is real is that God is God. In Revelation 5, the God who is seated on the throne is holding a scroll. The scroll is sealed with seven seals, and it seems to tell the story of reality: who God is and what God has done, is doing, and will do to defeat the forces of death and destruction as God redeems and remakes creation. But no one is worthy to take the scroll, to break its seals, and to read the story. "No one in heaven or on earth or under the earth"—no angel, no worshiper, no apostle, and no saint—"was able to open the scroll or to look into it" (5:3). "No one was found worthy," and John "began to weep" (5:4). The second reality is revealed. If the first reality is God is God (Rev. 4), the second reality is only God is God: nothing in all creation is the Creator (Rev. 5).

This double revelation of the real leaves John weeping. But then comes the revelation of Jesus Christ. As John weeps, another one of those who were unworthy comes to him and says, "Weep no more; behold, the Lion of the tribe of Judah, the Root of David, has conquered" (5:5). John looks and behold, the Lamb: "I saw a Lamb standing, as though it had been slain" (5:6). This lion who is the slain lamb takes the scroll, and John hears a "new song": "Worthy is the Lamb who was slain, for by his blood he has redeemed for God a people from every tribe, every tongue, language, and people" (5:8–9, AT). Revelation 14 repeats the language of throne, lamb, and new song. In this scene, the "redeemed" (14:4) are "with the Lamb" and they are his people: "his name and his Father's name" are "written on their foreheads" (14:1).

God is God. Only God is God. The Lamb who was slain is worthy. Because of the Lamb the unworthy worshipers are God's people. This is what is real. The difference and distinction between Creator and creatures are not finally a separating divide because the Lamb who was slain has "redeemed" and reconciled us to the "holy, holy, holy" Lord. The movement is from revealed unworthiness to honest weeping to redeemed worship: "every creature in heaven and on earth and under the earth and in the sea" sings, "To him who sits on the throne and to the Lamb be blessing and honor and glory and might forever and ever" (5:13).

This is the reality Revelation reveals, and the past, present, and future it portrays promise the victory of the Lamb. This victory turns upside down usual assumptions and practices of power. The Roman Empire, like powers past and present, is akin to the beast that imprisons through violence and achieves what it calls peace only by killing and enslaving. It "makes war" and demands "worship" (13:7–8), and it presents itself as "the great city" (17:18; compare Virgil's *Aeneid* 1.236–37; 4.232). In Revelation, by contrast, the Lamb is a king who makes peace, not by killing, but by being killed. This Lord redeems, not by enslaving, but by setting free. The surprise of this redemption and this rule is also a revelation: the real and final enemy is not the passing earthly powers but the dragon, the serpent of old, the darkness and chaos (Rev. 12–13). The song that celebrates that God's creatures are made "people for God" by the blood of the Lamb (5:9) is also an announcement that the forces of chaos, destruction, and death are overcome and vanquished (Rev. 20). The God who is not us, in freedom and grace, will be God with us. Creator and creature are reconciled in the Lamb—the slain Alpha and Omega, the worthy Creator who bleeds as a creature—and nothing, not even the dragon or beast or the earthly powers or death, can thwart God's creative and redeeming determination to be God with us. The enemy is defeated (20:7–11), God's righteousness reigns (20:11–15), God's beloved and delivered creatures feast with and live with the Lord (19:6–10; chaps. 21–22).

The unrolling of and looking into the scrolls indicate an order and care that testify to God's providence. Seven seals and seven bowls and seven trumpets and a thousand years proclaim a creation, a history, and a redemption in which even the chaos, conflict, and confusion are outcontrolled and overcome by the one who sits on the throne and by the Lamb. The details of image and symbol in Revelation, sometimes monstrous and sometimes paradisical, are often hard to interpret. But its forceful and fundamental message is unambiguous: God in Christ is victorious over sin, the enemy, and death. The headline news of Revelation is about who God is and what this God has done, is doing, and will do. God has and will redeem. God has and will set free. God has and will raise the dead. The Lamb has conquered, and God will establish new heavens and a new earth, a new city with a new garden. The sin, death, and curse that exiled God's children from Eden in Genesis will give way to a redemption and return, to new-creation life with God in the new garden city. Creation's river flows and the tree of life is forever planted and yielding fruit in the remade garden (22:1–2). The darkness and watery chaos is banished, and in the new Jerusalem shadows and threat are no more (21:1, 25; 22:25) because the presence of God is light and love (21:23; 22:5).

In the revelation of Jesus Christ, the one who is "the beginning and the end" is both the beginning and end of history. From garden and river to a new garden and river. From the tree of life to the tree of life. Between and binding this beginning and this end is a tree that the Romans used for death: the cross. The Lamb was slain. But that death, by the deep mystery of God's mercy, is the tree of life. Echoing Jesus's words from the cross in John 19:30, "It is finished," Revelation envisions the Lamb, slain but then seated and saying: "It is done" (Rev. 21:6). As John sees the new heaven and the new earth, he also hears "a loud voice from the throne saying, 'Behold, the dwelling place of God is with [humanity]. He will dwell with them, and they will be his people, and God himself will be with them as their God. He will wipe away every tear from their eyes, and death shall be no more, neither shall there be mourning, nor crying, nor pain anymore, for the former things have passed away" (21:1–4). The defeat of death; the overcoming of chaos; the end of the enemy; redemption from sin; the togetherness of an undivided "we" from every tribe, tongue, and people; and God's "no more" to sorrow and suffering: "It is done." Revelation reveals this Lamb, the one who was and is and is to come, the first and the last, the beginning and the end, the one who made peace by his blood, the one who is worthy, the one who says, "Fear not, I am." It is in singing to and beholding this slain "Lamb of God, who takes away the sin of the world" (John 1:29) that Revelation ends, "Amen. Come, Lord Jesus" (Rev. 22:20).

PART 3

Case Study and Synthesis

CHAPTER 7

Paul's Letter to the Romans

IN THE LATE FOURTH CENTURY, SOMEONE READ Romans. "Holy Scripture," as George Herbert writes, is "the well / That washes what it shows," the living and active word that both reveals and redeems as it unearths honest need and forgives and sets free in Jesus. This happened for the fourth-century reader, Saint Augustine: educated yet somewhat empty; philosophically, culturally, and even religiously experienced but still restless. Then came a voice: "Take up and read." What he read was Romans. What this word worked as he read Romans was an exposure and understanding of his restlessness, and also the gift of forgiving and peace-creating love through Jesus Christ (Augustine's *Confessions*). This history of reading Romans tends to repeat. Martin Luther, in 1545, remembered that thirty years before, as he "pounded on Paul" in Romans 1:17, his reading—and life—shifted from hating what he thought was "the righteous God who punishes sinners" to loving the one Romans reveals as the God who, in mercy and grace, gives righteousness and life "as a gift" (*Preface to Collected Latin Writings*). John Wesley, a minister of the eighteenth century, encountered the gospel proclaimed in and through Romans as forgiveness and freedom: "I felt my heart strangely warmed. I felt I did trust in Christ, Christ alone for salvation, and an assurance was given me that he had taken away my sins, even mine" (*Journals and Diaries*). As a hymn his brother

Charles Wesley sings, "My chains feel off, my heart was free. . . . No condemnation now I dread; / Jesus, and all in Him, is mine" (Charles Wesley, "And Can It Be That I Should Gain?").

Like the voice Augustine heard, these stories are an invitation: take up and read—Romans.

—

Paul's apostolic pattern means that most of his letters are written to communities he established and knew. Paul traveled to a city, proclaimed "the word of the cross," moved to another city to

63 BC	Romans gain control of Judea
44 BC	Julius Caesar is assassinated
37–4 BC	Herod the Great serves as king of Judea
27 BC	Octavian (or Augustus) becomes the first Roman emperor
ca. 7–4 BC	Jesus is born prior to the death of Herod the Great
AD 26–36	Pontius Pilate serves as governor of Judea
ca. AD 30	Pontius Pilate orders Jesus's crucifixion
ca. AD 32–35	Saul (or Paul) has a vision of Jesus while traveling to Damascus
ca. AD 46–49	Christian leaders gather in Jerusalem to discuss Gentile conversion
AD 49	Emperor Claudius expels Jews from Rome
AD 50–52	Paul spreads Christianity in Corinth
AD 50s–60s	Paul writes numerous letters to Christian congregations
AD 64	Nero persecutes Christians in Rome (Peter & Paul possibly martyred)
ca. AD 65–90	The Gospels are written
AD 66–73	The Jewish War with Rome erupts
AD 70	The Romans sack Jerusalem and destroy the temple

First Century BC and AD Dates

preach again, and occasioned by various crises and needs, wrote pastoral letters back to the churches, preaching afresh the gospel he had first announced. Romans is different. Paul had not, as he says in Romans 1:15, "proclaimed the gospel also to you who are in Rome" (AT). Rather than being a letter back to a church where Paul has preached the gospel, Romans is a letter ahead to a city where and beyond which he hopes to preach the gospel. According to Romans 15, after Paul's extensive travel and ministry in the eastern Mediterranean, he intends to go to Jerusalem and then move west to Rome and from there to Spain in order to "preach the gospel, not where Christ has already been named" (15:18–29). Acts narrates Paul's arrival in Jerusalem, but this arrival is met with arrest and an imprisonment that eventually finds Paul in Rome (Acts 21–28). Imprisonment is not the end of Paul's preaching. Letters from prison continue to proclaim Christ to various churches and, as one epistle puts it, "I am bound in chains, but the word of God is not bound" (2 Tim. 2:9, AT).

Rather than a letter of pastoral intervention and repreaching, Romans is a letter of apostolic introduction and initial preaching. Romans 16 indicates that Paul's relational network overlaps with some of those who are in Rome, and some of what he writes, in Romans 14, for example, suggests an awareness of the questions and tensions present

Rom. 1:1–15	Letter opening: introduction and greetings
Rom. 1:16–17	Summary of the gospel
Rom. 1:18–3:20	The revelation of human unrighteousness
Rom. 3:21–4:25	The revelation of God's righteousness
Rom. 5:1–8:39	Deepening the diagnosis and the good news
Rom. 9:1–11:36	What does the gospel mean for Israel?
Rom. 12:1–15:21	The gospel on the ground
Rom. 15:22–16:27	Letter closing: plans and final greetings

Structure of Romans

among "those in Rome who are loved by God" (Rom. 1:7). Romans, however, is a letter of introduction, an indication of Paul's plans—to preach the gospel in Spain—and an introduction to Paul's gospel—"the power of God for salvation" (1:16). That Paul does not introduce himself by way of autobiography is theologically significant. He introduces himself and his desire to proclaim the gospel by introducing and proclaiming the gospel. Romans 1:15 says, "I am eager to preach the gospel to you also who are in Rome." Romans does just that: it preaches the gospel of God's Son (1:1–3).

Paul's proclamation unfolds in stages, sometimes circling back to dig deeper and declare again the gospel, sometimes asking and exploring the questions evoked by this proclamation or experienced by those in Rome.

Romans 1:1–15 is the letter opening, both including an introduction and indicating the content of what Paul calls "the gospel . . . about God's Son" (1:1–3). This gospel is then spoken again in Romans 1:16–17 as the revelation of "the righteousness of God" and the "power of God for salvation": "For I am not ashamed of the gospel, because it is the power of God for salvation to everyone who believes: to the Jew first, and also to the Greek. For in the gospel the righteousness of God is revealed—a righteousness that is from faith and for faith, as it is written: 'The one who is righteous by faith will live'" (AT). Romans 1:18–3:20 reveals human unrighteousness, and Romans 3:21–31 announces "the redemption that is in Christ Jesus" that reveals God's righteousness (Romans 4 discovers this creative, saving, and resurrecting righteousness in the Genesis narrative about Abraham). Romans 5–8 deepens the diagnosis of human bondage and need even as it explores and proclaims again the grace and love of God in Jesus Christ: "For I am sure that neither death nor life, nor angels nor rulers, nor things present nor things to come, nor powers, nor height nor depth, nor anything else in all creation, will be able to separate us from the love of God in Christ Jesus our Lord" (8:38–39). Romans 9–11 asks a painful, honest, and finally hopeful question: Does Israel's current rejection of Jesus as messiah and Lord entail God's rejection of Israel? Paul's no explores the word of God that has not failed in past, present, and future tenses and concludes with an unveiling of the mystery of mercy (11:32) that gives way to worship:

> Oh, the depth of the riches and wisdom and knowledge of God! How unsearchable are his judgments and how inscrutable his ways!
>
> "For who has known the mind of the Lord,
>   or who has been his counselor?"
> "Or who has given a gift to him
>   that he might be repaid?"
>
> For from him and through him and to him are all things. To him be glory forever. Amen. (11:33–36)

In Romans 12:1–15:21, Paul considers how the good news of God's grace in Jesus both creates and characterizes a surprising community that crosses boundaries and, despite persisting differences, embodies unity through a culturally transgressive love that seeks to honor others and welcome each as one for whom Christ died. Romans 15:22–16:25 concludes the letter, communicating Paul's intentions and hopes (Jerusalem, then Rome, then Spain) and sharing greetings.

Romans 1–3

Romans 1 introduces the letter by introducing the gospel. As Paul insists, he is "an apostle, set apart for the gospel of God," and so is "eager to preach the gospel" and is "not ashamed of the gospel" (1:1, 15–16). Romans 1:1–4 provides an initial definition and declaration of this gospel: "The gospel of God, which he promised beforehand through his prophets in the holy Scriptures, concerning his Son, who was descended from David according to the flesh and was declared to be the Son of God in power according to the Spirit of holiness by his resurrection from the dead, Jesus Christ our Lord" (1:1–4). The gospel of God is the gospel about God's Son. This Son is a descendant of David according to the flesh: an Israelite with a royal lineage. This Son is also Son of God, a name designated by resurrection: this Son died; this Son lives. The gospel is about this Son: descended from David and declared Son of God, crucified and risen, the Son who is Jesus Christ our Lord.

Paul begins with this revelation: to speak the gospel is to tell the story of this Son, to proclaim the good news about Jesus Christ.

This story and this Son, as Romans 1:16–17 indicates, is the promise of the gospel that is the power of God for salvation: "For I am not ashamed of the gospel, for it is the power of God for salvation to everyone who believes, to the Jew first and also to the Greek. For in it the righteousness of God is revealed from faith for faith, as it is written, 'The righteous shall live by faith.'" Who? Jesus. What? The power of God for salvation. For whom? Everyone.

Paul begins with this revelation: to speak the gospel is to tell the story of this Son, to proclaim the good news about Jesus Christ.

This "for everyone" emphasis is a refrain in Romans. Paul consistently attends to the particular inheritances and histories of peoples—of Jew and gentile—even as he announces a fundamental solidarity of human need and human hope: "there is no distinction," both because "all have sinned" (3:22–23) and because "all who call on the name of the Lord will be saved" (10:12–13, AT). Christ as Lord of *all* is the horizon of history: "Christ became servant to Israel in order to confirm the promises to the patriarchs and so that gentiles might glorify God for this mercy" (15:8–13, AT); "to this end Christ died and lived again, that he might be Lord both of the dead and of the living" (14:9).

Together, Romans 1:1–4 and 1:16–17 define and declare the gospel: the gospel is about God's crucified and risen Son, and the gospel is the revelation of God's saving power. The gospel is the story of Jesus—the Savior; the gospel is the promise that gives Jesus—and saves. In the words of 1 Corinthians 15:1–4, "the gospel . . . by which you are being saved" is the glad and grace-giving news "that Christ died for our sins in accordance with the Scriptures, that he was buried, that he was raised on the third day in accordance with the Scriptures." To borrow a Pauline summary of the Pauline gospel: "Christ Jesus came into the world to save sinners" (1 Tim. 1:15).

Paul is not ashamed of this saving news that proclaims and gives the crucified and risen Son of God because, as he says in Romans 1:17, "the righteousness of God is revealed" in it. The gospel of God reveals the righteousness of God. Paul returns to this theme in Romans 3:21. What Romans 1:18–3:20 reveals, however, is human unrighteousness: "God's wrath is revealed from heaven against all the ungodliness and unrighteousness of human beings" (1:18, AT). Paul is an apostle of a double apocalypse, a twofold revelation. Romans reveals both human unrighteousness (1:18) and God's righteousness (3:21). To return to some lines from W. H. Auden, "nothing can save us that is possible: / we who must die demand a miracle" (*For the Time Being*). Romans reveals both this "we who must die" and the "miracle" beyond the "possible." Just as the gospel is God's power for salvation to all, both Jew and gentile (1:16), the revelation of unrighteousness diagnoses all, both Jew and gentile. In the summative words of Romans 3:22–23 and 3:9, "there is no distinction, for all have sinned," and "all, both Jews and gentiles, are under sin" (AT).

Romans 1:18–3:20 announces that all humanity is included in the history of idolatry and immorality. It is a history of human unrighteousness from which not even Israel is immune. Paul refers to patterns of "exchanging the glory of the immortal God for mortal images" (1:23, AT) and those who "worshiped and served the creature rather than the Creator" (1:25), worship that echoes both the rebellion of Eden (Gen. 3) and Israel's golden calf idolatry at Mount Sinai (Exod. 32). Confirming this expansive indictment, Romans 3:10–18 quotes several passages from the Old Testament:

> "None is righteous, no, not one;
> no one understands;
> no one seeks for God.
> All have turned aside; together they have become worthless;
> no one does good,
> not even one."

This diagnosis is deeper than any human divide: beneath every "us and them" there is the "we" of human bondage, sin, and death. The novel *Don Quixote* hits this bedrock: "What is called need is found everywhere, and extends to all places, and reaches everyone" (Cervantes, *Don Quixote*) "Lift every roof," writes Thornton Wilder, "and you will find seven puzzled hearts" (*The Woman of Andros*).

For Paul, this reality requires revelation. God speaks so that human sin can be seen. Romans 3:19–20 identifies and announces this need-unveiling, honesty-evoking, death-diagnosing word of God: "Now we know that whatever the law says it speaks to those who are under the law, so that every mouth may be stopped, and the whole world may be held accountable to God. For by works of the law no human being will be righteous before God, since through the law comes knowledge of sin" (AT). God's law speaks so mouths may be stopped and sin might be seen. Romans 7:12 insists and confesses that the law of God is "holy and righteous and good." The law describes what is holy, good, and righteous; the law diagnoses what is unholy, not good, and unrighteous. According to Paul, the law is righteous (7:12) but righteousness is not through the law (Gal. 2:21; 3:21). What the law is, is God's good commandments (see Rom. 7). What the law does, according to Romans, is reveal sin (3:20), work wrath (4:15), increase the trespass (5:20), and show sin to be sin (7:13). The law does not remove sin; it reveals sin. The law does not deliver us from our need; the law diagnoses us in our need. Genesis 3 narrates the origin of life according to the lie: "you will be like God" and "you will not die." The law is the truth louder than the lie: "I am the LORD your God" (Exod. 20:2), and you are "dead in [your] trespasses and sins" (Eph. 2:1).

It is at this site of revealed human unrighteousness that Paul returns to and proclaims God's merciful righteousness. To quote W. H. Auden once more, it is "just here, among the ruins and the bones, that we may rejoice in the perfected work which is not ours" (*The Sea and the Mirror*). The apparent dead-end of "no human being will be righteous" (Rom. 3:20, AT) is a grave that gives way to the resurrecting word of God's righteousness: "But now . . ." (3:21). Perhaps the "possible" cannot save the "we who must die." But God's righteousness and grace in Christ are mercy and "miracle": righteousness given at the site of sin; life summoned at the site of death.

> But now, apart from the law, the righteousness of God has been made manifest, to which the Law and the Prophets testify. This righteousness is given through faith in Jesus Christ to all who believe. There is no difference between Jew and gentile, for all have sinned and fall short of the glory of God, and all are justified freely by his grace through the redemption that came by Christ Jesus. God presented Christ as a sacrifice of atonement, through the shedding of his blood—to be received by faith. He did this to demonstrate his righteousness, because in his forbearance he had left the sins committed beforehand unpunished—he did it to demonstrate his righteousness at the present time, so as to be just and the one who justifies those who have faith in Jesus. (3:21–26, AT)

This is a dense passage, but attending to the details is to hear both disjunction with what has come before and the drama at the center of all things. According to Romans 3:20, by works of law no one will be declared righteous. "But now," interrupts Romans 3:21, "apart from the law, the righteousness of God has been made manifest." This revelation of righteousness, however, does not result in the "none are righteous" condemnation suggested by Romans 3:9–20. The merciful surprise is that God's righteousness breaks into the world of "all have sinned" (3:23) and yet—somehow, strangely, by grace—creates a new reality of "and are righteous" (3:24). This out-of-the-opposite righteousness, according to Paul, is embodied and effected through the "grace that is the redemption that is in Christ Jesus" (3:24, AT). The language Paul uses in Romans 3:24–25—the language of redemption and sacrifice—indicates that Jesus's death is both deliverance from bondage and final atonement for sin. Together with the language of righteousness that has been repeated since Romans 1:17, these words become the way Paul, in Romans 3:21–26, declares "the word of the cross": God has acted in Jesus to set captives free, to forgive sin, and to make all things right.

Romans 3:21–26 both begins and ends with the announcement of God's righteousness. Genesis 18:25 asks a fundamental question: "Will not the judge of all the earth do right?" (AT). For Paul, the gospel announces the answer in the present tense: in Jesus Christ, the judge of all the earth has done right. This still has a future dimension for Paul, as he anticipates a "day of the Lord" (1 Thess. 5:2) and a "judgment seat of Christ" (2 Cor. 5:10; Rom. 14) at which all will be made right. A move from future to present, however, can be traced from Romans 2 to Romans 3. In Romans 2, "God's righteous judgment" is on the horizon; it is something that "will be revealed" (2:5). The "but now" of Romans 3:21, however, proclaims that revelation as the present: the righteousness of God is manifest. In contrast to the future in which "no one will be declared righteous," the present reality is that the "all have sinned" are, now, "declared righteous." If the basis for the future judgment was "works of the law" (3:20) or "God will repay each according to their works" (2:6, AT), the grounds for the present judgment is "grace"—it is "the redemption that is in Christ Jesus" (3:24). To translate the terms, the value of and verdict on a human life are not an uncertain judgment decided in the future on the basis of a person's biography; rather, the value of and verdict on a human life are the firm foundation declared in the present on the basis of the gift of Jesus Christ.

Paul's vocabulary of righteousness conjures up a scene of final judgment. Following his word-images, perhaps it is possible to imagine standing in a long and winding line, awaiting your turn to appear before the judge of all the earth. God begins to make a thorough review of your life so a value and verdict can be rendered. Perhaps there is a book or a biopic. Either way, there is your biography: what you have done and what you have left undone, what you have thought and what you said. It is your life: the good, the bad, the ups and downs, the love, the hate, the anger, the joy, the tears, the laughter, the deceit, the doubt, the compassion, the despair, the hope, the hurts. "None is righteous" (Rom. 3:10), the judge of all the earth will do right (Gen. 18:25), and so, "by works of law no one will be declared righteous before God" (Rom. 3:20, AT).

But now. . . . Rewind, reread, replay. You are before the judge and the biography is about to be read. The book opens and behold: A baby born among animals. A friend of tax collectors and sinners, one who came to heal the sick, comfort the suffering, liberate the enslaved, forgive the unrighteous. This one travels to Jerusalem, where he is joyfully welcomed, only to be betrayed, arrested, tried, mocked, crucified, and buried. But burial is not the end of this biography: the stone is rolled away, the tomb is empty, and this Jesus is risen from the dead. This life, this death, this resurrection, the life of the one who is seated at God's right hand (Rom. 8:34), the life of the one God did not spare but sent (Rom. 8:32), the life of the one who loved me and gave himself for me (Gal. 2:20): this one reveals the righteousness of God; this one is the righteousness of God (1 Cor. 1:30); in this one we "become the righteousness of God" (2 Cor. 5:21). As Colossians 3:3 declares, "Our life is hidden with God in Christ" (AT). What God sees and says when God looks at you is grounded in the gift of Jesus Christ: "You are," God says, "righteous, you are redeemed, you are forgiven, you are—forever and finally—my beloved child."

This righteousness is revealed "apart from the law" and at the open wound of shared human need: all sinned (Rom. 3:20, 23). The grace given in the gospel, in other words, is not conditioned by the various criteria cultures use to measure worth and draw lines between us and them. "Apart from law" and "all sinned" indicate a grace that is not contained within the boundary drawn by the possession or performance of the law: boasting is "excluded" because a person "is justified by faith apart from works of the law" (3:27–28). This boast-excluding and boundary-exploding grace translates into the proclamation of one gospel for all (1:16) and one God of all. "God is one," declaring righteous all who sinned—Jew and gentile—through the grace that gives Jesus (3:30).

What God sees and says when God looks at you is grounded in the gift of Jesus Christ: "You are," God says, "righteous, you are redeemed, you are forgiven, you are—forever and finally—my beloved child."

The gospel about Jesus that is the power of God that gives Jesus is revelation and reality: at the site of sin, bondage, and death God in Christ has created righteousness, freedom, and life. This forgiving and life-giving mercy is not based on a person's biography; it is grounded and given in the grace that is God's Son, Jesus Christ.

Romans 4–8

In Romans 5–8, Paul returns to and deepens the diagnosis of human need; he also returns to and announces again the liberating grace of God in Jesus Christ.

The next section will open with Romans 9, where Paul asks after God's promises in relation to Israel. That story starts with Isaac in Romans 9:7, but Isaac's father, Abraham, is already the focus in Romans 4. Paul's insistent proclamation in Romans 3:21–31 is that the one God relates to and declares righteous all people not on the basis of the possession or performance of the law but on the grounds of the gift of Jesus Christ. To summarize with the imagery from our previous section, the value of and verdict on a human life are not an uncertain future judgment rendered on the basis of a person's biography. Rather, the value of and verdict on a human person are an already-spoken promise declared in the life, death, and life again of Jesus Christ: righteous, forgiven, set free, God's beloved child. This "gospel of God," according to Paul, was "promised beforehand through [God's] prophets in the holy Scriptures" (Rom. 1:2). In Romans 4, Paul reads the Genesis narrative about Abraham as a witness to the God who always operates according to this surprising grace: God justifies the ungodly, God calls into being that which does not exist, God raises the dead (4:5, 17).

Let's start with a surprise: "The law was brought in so that trespasses might increase. But where sin increased, grace increased all the more" (5:20, AT). This repeats a distinction: the purpose of the law is not to remove or deliver us from sin; the law reveals and diagnoses sin. What is strange and startling—the surprise—is the triple image of increase. The law increased the trespass; sin increased; grace increased all the more. Grace is given at the site of sin, but grace, not sin, is most bountiful, more fundamental and final.

But this raises a question: "What shall we say then? Shall we go on sinning so that grace may abound?" (6:1, AT). If an abundance of sin entails a superabundance of grace (5:20), shall we continue to sin in order to increase grace? Paul asks and answers this question in Romans 6: "Shall we go on sinning so that grace may abound? By no means!"—Absolutely not! Don't even imagine it! (6:1–2).

This might seem like a time for footnotes and caveats, a moment to indicate that grace does, after all, come with a few conditions and qualifications. Perhaps the gas pedal of the gospel had Paul over the theological speed limit, and he now needs to tap the brakes and add an "if." In fact, Paul's honest question about the increase of sin and grace unfolds as a kind of acceleration or, to mix the metaphor, a deeper diagnosis of human need and a radical redeclaration of God's grace. Shall we continue in sin? Paul asks. Romans 6:2–4 begins the answer: "By no means! How can we who died to sin still live in it? Do you not know that all of us who have been baptized into Christ Jesus were baptized into his death? We were buried therefore with him by baptism into death, in order that, just as Christ was raised from the dead by the glory of the Father, we too might walk in newness of life." This deepening of sin and grace in relation to the realities of death and life continues in Romans 6:5, "For if we have been united with him in a death like his, we shall certainly be united with him in a resurrection like his." This becomes a refrain: "our old self was crucified with him" (6:6); "anyone who has died has been freed from sin" (6:7, AT); "if we have died with Christ, we will also live with him" (6:8, AT); "in the same way, count yourself dead to sin, but alive to God" (6:11, AT).

Paul's answer is an announcement: you have died with and in Christ. This death with and life in Christ are an end and a new creation: you are no longer "under the law" but "under grace"; sin is not your lord—it does not have "dominion" over you and you are not its "slave"—because your life is given "in Christ Jesus our Lord"—you are "bound to God" and "servants of righteousness" (6:14–23). This reality is mystery, mercy, and miracle. Paul does not so much explain it as proclaim it: you have died with Christ and your life is in Christ. According to Paul, "bondage to sin leads to death" (6:16, AT). But out of death, from being buried with Christ, flows "the free gift of God [that] is eternal life in Christ Jesus our Lord" (6:23).

Death and life also dominate Romans 7. Human life "under the law" (6:14) is portrayed with power and personal resonance:

> We know that the law is spiritual; but I am unspiritual, sold as a slave to sin. I do not understand what I do. For what I want to do I do not do, but what I hate I do. And if I do what I do not want to do, I agree that the law is good. As it is, it is no longer I myself who do it, but it is sin living in me. For I know that good itself does not dwell in me, that is, in my sinful nature. For I have the desire to do what is good, but I cannot carry it out. For I do not do the good I want to do, but the evil I do not want to do—this I keep on doing. (7:14–19, AT)

This description of doubleness, confusion, and inability captures the pattern of human history and human life. Sin seizes "an opportunity through the commandment" (7:11) and, paradoxically, "through what is good" and promises life, produces death. In this way, according to Paul, "sin [is] shown to be sin" (7:13)—bondage and need and incapacity are unearthed, rendered acute, and are seen and break the surface as an honest cry: "Who will deliver me from this body of death?" (7:24). Paul's answer, mercifully but still surprisingly, is that we are delivered from this death by death: "So, my brothers and sisters, you also died to the law through the body of Christ, that you might belong to another who was raised from the dead in order that we might bear fruit for God" (7:4, AT). The law, it seems, only has jurisdiction over the living. Freedom from death and forgiveness from sin are, as Romans announces, realities that go through and come out of death—they are resurrection: "you . . . belong to another . . . who has been raised from the dead." To the question, "Who will deliver me?" Paul declares, "Thanks be to God through Jesus Christ our Lord. . . . There is therefore now no condemnation for those who are in Christ Jesus" (7:25–8:1).

According to this one and only gospel of God's love and grace in Jesus, the way God redeems and restores us—however mysterious, however miraculous, and also however merciful—is not by ensuring that we survive what we call salvation. Redemption is not realizing our potential or moving from being mixed up to being straightened out. In Christ, we go, by grace, into and out of the grave.

In Romans 8, this contrast between life "under law" that is "death" (6:14, 16) and life "under grace" that is raised out of death with Christ (6:4–11, 14) is described in terms of a contrast between the unto-death-life "according to flesh" and the out-of-death-life "according to the Spirit." "For those who live according to the flesh set their minds on the things of the flesh, but those who live according to the Spirit set their minds on the things of the Spirit. For to set the mind on the flesh is death, but to set the mind on the Spirit is life and peace" (8:5–6). This pattern of living, life according to the Spirit, is life after (and out of) death with Christ. As 2 Corinthians 5:14 proclaims, "one has died for all, therefore all have died." Or consider Paul's confession in Galatians 2:20, "I have been crucified with Christ, and I no longer live, but Christ lives in me" (AT). According to this one and only gospel of God's love and grace in Jesus, the way God redeems and restores us—however mysterious, however miraculous, and also however merciful—is not by ensuring that we survive what we call salvation. Redemption is not realizing our potential or moving from being mixed up to being straightened out. In Christ, we go, by grace, into and out of the grave. The pattern of redeeming, creating, and life-giving grace is not just getting better, getting clean, or getting well—it is *death* and *resurrection* in the crucified and risen Christ. We may not, in this sense, survive our own salvation, but we live as those who are forever loved on the other side of death because grace has opened the grave.

The upside-down-ness of this invites repetition. The language of death and life that dominates Romans 5–8, together with the revelation of righteousness in the "now" of Jesus's death and resurrection announced in Romans 3–5, combines to proclaim a merciful surprise. What Paul calls life "under law" (Rom. 6) or "according to the flesh" (Rom. 8) or "in Adam" (Rom. 5) is a bondage unto death because it is life with death and judgment ahead of us. "But now," Paul might say, life "under grace" (6:14) or "according to the Spirit" (Rom. 8) or "in Christ" (Rom. 5) is freedom and aliveness because death and judgment are behind us: God has spoken his word of righteousness, not on the basis of your biography but in and as the gift of Jesus crucified and risen; you have been buried with Christ and made alive in Christ out of his empty tomb. Even as Paul faces and feels "the sufferings of this present time" (8:18) and hears creation and human creatures groaning for redemption and resurrection (8:19–23), his final song is a nothing-can-separate-us love:

> What then shall we say to these things? If God is for us, who can be against us? He who did not spare his own Son but gave

> him up for us all, how will he not also with him graciously give us all things? Who shall bring any charge against God's elect? It is God who justifies. Who is to condemn? Christ Jesus is the one who died—more than that, who was raised—who is at the right hand of God, who indeed is interceding for us. Who shall separate us from the love of Christ? Shall tribulation, or distress, or persecution, or famine, or nakedness, or danger, or sword? As it is written,
>
> "For your sake we are being killed all the day long;
> we are regarded as sheep to be slaughtered."
>
> No, in all these things we are more than conquerors through him who loved us. For I am sure that neither death nor life, nor angels nor rulers, nor things present nor things to come, nor powers, nor height nor depth, nor anything else in all creation, will be able to separate us from the love of God in Christ Jesus our Lord. (8:31–39)

Paul can make this kind of unshakable confession because the final questions about the future, about death and judgment, are no longer future questions; they are "*It is finished*" questions. "There is therefore now no condemnation for those who are in Christ Jesus" (8:1). "Who is to condemn? Christ Jesus is the one who died—more than that, who was raised—who is at the right hand of God, who indeed is interceding for us" (8:34). The Spirit who "pours this love into our hearts" (5:5, AT) sings a song not of fear but of adoption: "the Spirit . . . bears witness . . . that we are children of God" (8:15–16). This relationship is our bedrock reality: we relate to God as "Abba! Father!" and God, in and through his eternal and coequal Son, addresses us as his forgiven and forever children: "You are my beloved child, in you I am well pleased."

Romans 5:1 opens with this already-spoken word of righteousness: having "been justified by faith, we have peace with God through our Lord Jesus Christ." The language of righteousness echoes the end of Romans 4. There, however, righteousness is tied to resurrection: God is "the one who raised from the dead Jesus our Lord, who was delivered up for our trespasses and raised for our righteousness" (4:24–25, AT). It is this God and this life-from-death grace that Paul discovers in the Genesis narrative about Abraham. The impossibility of God's promise is emphasized in Genesis. When God tells the aged Abraham that he will have a child with barren Sarah, Abraham laughs (Gen. 17), and when the cannot-be promise comes to pass, Sarah laughs again (Gen. 21). Paul, in Romans, hears this promise beyond the possible as itself promising the final impossibility of grace: resurrection. Abraham's faith, as Paul interprets it, is "hope against hope" (Rom. 4:18): Abraham's body was "dead" and Sarah's womb was "dead" (4:19), and therefore the birth of Isaac was life from death. Abraham trusted the God who, by grace, empties graves, who, as Paul puts it, "gives life to the dead and calls into being that which is not" (4:17, AT), the God who "raised from the dead Jesus our Lord" (4:24).

This life-out-of-death pattern—resurrection and empty grave—shapes Paul's proclamation of righteousness and grace. According to Romans 4:5, the God who creates from nothing and raises the dead (4:17) is also the one "who justifies the ungodly." At the site of nonexistence, death, and sin, God calls into being, makes alive, and declares righteous. This, for Paul, is the pattern of grace: not wages for work (4:4) but the forgiveness of sins (4:6–7). Grace, as it is revealed in Christ and as Paul discovers it in (and beyond) Genesis, is not a gift that corresponds to a given reality; grace contradicts the old and as the power of God creates something new: freedom from bondage, hope from despair, strength in weakness, love from aloneness, life from death.

This surprising and out-of-the-opposite grace is given dramatic expression in Romans 5. Paul offers an extended contrast between Adam and Jesus in which the language of "gift" is prominent.

> Therefore, just as sin came into the world through one man, and death through sin, and so death spread to all men because all sinned—for sin indeed was in the world before the law was given, but sin is not counted where there is no law. Yet death reigned from Adam to Moses, even over those whose sinning was not like the transgression of Adam, who was a type of the one who was to come. But the free gift is not like the trespass. For if many died through one man's trespass, much more have the grace of God and the free gift by the grace of that one man Jesus Christ abounded for many. And the free gift is not like the result of that one man's sin. For the judgment following one trespass brought condemnation, but the free gift following many trespasses brought justification. For if, because of one man's trespass, death reigned through that one man, much more will those who receive the abundance of grace and the free gift of righteousness reign in life through the one man Jesus Christ. (5:12–17).

According to this contrast, Christ overcomes and undoes and goes beyond Adam's transgression. Through Adam sin and death enter and reign; through Jesus, after and out of sin and death, come righteousness and life. This, to quote Paul's terms, is "the grace of God and the free gift by . . . grace": the gift of Christ given where there was sin and death; the gift of Christ that gives righteousness and life.

This mismatch between God's grace and those who receive it stands out and is surprising in Paul's religious and social contexts. "Grace" is the ordinary word for a gift, favor, or benefit. These terms (*charis* in Greek or *donum* in Latin) are common in both Greco-Roman and Jewish literature. They both describe ordinary, everyday social interactions and celebrate divine generosity. The taken-for-granted pattern of gift giving was that a good gift is a benefit or favor given to a person who was, in some sense, worthy to receive it. Worth or fittingness might be measured in social, religious, economic, political, or moral terms. Whatever tokens of value, metrics of fittingness, or criteria of worth, however, a gift was a good and a real gift when and where there was a match or correspondence between the gift and the worth of the recipient. Two near contemporaries of Paul in the first century AD expressed this "normal grace." Seneca, a Roman statesmen and philosopher, wrote a handbook on gift giving entitled *On Benefits,* which insists we should "pick out those who are worthy of receiving our gifts" (*On Benefits* 1.1.2). Philo of Alexandria, a Jewish author writing in Greek from Egypt, calls God "gift loving" and notes that this God gives "not as a payment" but as "a gift" to those "considered worthy" (*On Moses* 2.242).

When Paul's letters are read in this context, the declaration that the gift of Christ is given to the unworthy—the bound, the sinner, the weak, the ungodly, the dead—is a surprise. Paul does not identify the correspondence between divine grace and human worth; rather, Paul announces the incongruity of God's gift and human worth. The language of gift or grace forms a refrain in Romans 5:12–21. This "grace of God" is "the free gift by the grace of the one man Jesus Christ," and it is given "after many trespasses" and where and when death and sin reign. The content and character of this gift is specified in Romans 5:6–10:

> For while we were still weak, at the right time Christ died for the ungodly. For one will scarcely die for a righteous person—though perhaps for a good person one would dare even to die—but God shows his love for us in that while we were still sinners, Christ died for us. Since, therefore, we have now been justified by his blood, much more shall we be saved by him from the wrath of God. For if while we were enemies we were reconciled to God by the death of his Son, much more, now that we are reconciled, shall we be saved by his life.

Notice the *what,* the *for whom,* and the *when* of God's love in Jesus. The gift God gave is "Christ died for us" (5:8). Grace—the gift narrated and promised in the gospel—is the Son God did not spare "but gave" (8:32); grace is "the Son of God, who loved me and gave himself for me" (Gal. 2:20). This "grace of God" is given "at the right time," "while we were still weak" (Rom. 5:6), and this gift that is God's love is given to and for the weak, the ungodly, the sinner, the enemy. Unlike the fitting gifts that characterize Paul's context, the gospel announces and gives the grace of God that does not require any already-existing worth.

God does not give the gift of Christ to those who are worthy; God gives the gift in Christ to those who are unworthy. This kind of gift giving was radical in Paul's cultural and religious context.

God does not give the gift of Christ to those who are worthy; God gives the gift in Christ to those who are unworthy. This kind of gift giving was radical in Paul's cultural and religious context.

God's love is not congruous; it is creative. As Martin Luther once wrote, "The love of God does not find but creates that which is pleasing to it" (*Heidelberg Disputation*). God's love that is the grace of God, confesses Romans 5:8, looks like this: "while we were still sinners, Christ died for us." This grace, incongruously, is given to the sinner, the bound, and the dead. This grace, impossibly, creates righteousness, freedom, and life. This is the grace of the God who, as Paul says, justifies the ungodly, gives life to the dead, and calls into being that which is not (4:5, 17). This is the grace of God in which "there is therefore now no condemnation" (8:1). This grace—the gift that is "Christ died for us"—is the love of God that Paul is sure nothing and no one can separate us from: "For I am sure that neither death nor life, nor angels nor rulers, nor things present nor things to come, nor powers, nor height nor depth, nor anything else in all creation, will be able to separate us from the love of God in Christ Jesus our Lord" (8:38–39).

Romans 9–11

Romans 8 ends in song: not death, not life, no one and nothing, can separate us from the love of God in Christ Jesus (8:38–39). We have died with Christ. The gift of Christ is given where there is sin and death and creates righteousness and life. In Christ, judgment and death are behind rather than ahead of us. This good news is the source of Paul's nothing-can-separate-us song.

As Romans 9 opens, however, that song turns to sorrow: "I speak the truth in Christ, I am not lying. My conscience confirms it through the Holy Spirit. I have great sorrow and unceasing anguish in my heart" (9:1–2, AT). The source of this sadness, according to Paul, is the confusing disjunction between Israel's irrevocable calling and many Israelites' rejection of Jesus the Messiah. Paul's anguish and Israel's graced history and inheritance come together in Romans 9:3–5: "For I could wish that I myself were cursed and cut off from Christ for the sake of my people, my kinsfolk according to the flesh, the people of Israel. Theirs is the adoption to sonship; theirs the divine glory, the covenants, the receiving of the law, the temple worship and the promises. Theirs are the patriarchs, and from them is traced the human ancestry of the Messiah, who is God over all, forever praised!" (AT). Jesus is the messiah of Israel, and yet many—most—Israelites have "stumbled over the stumbling stone" by not receiving and recognizing Jesus as "Lord," as "the end of the law unto righteousness" (9:32–10:4).

Romans 9–11 speaks from this pain (9:1–5); it speaks in and as prayer (10:1); and Paul's honesty and finally Paul's hope are written out of this open wound. That this pain is held by a deeper promise is expressed in the question with a definite negative answer in Romans 9:6: "Has the word of God failed—no!" (AT). Romans 9–11 traces the history of God's unfailing word in past, present, and future tenses. The horizon is finally one of hope—God will have mercy on all (11:32)—because, as Paul discovers and declares, God was and is and will be the God who has mercy.

Romans 9:7 picks up Israel's story where Romans 4 left off. Romans 4 remembers the birth of Isaac and reads it as resurrection. Romans 9 identifies Isaac as a child of God not according to the flesh but born by the promise. In Romans 4, Abraham's "hope against hope" is trust in the God "who justifies the ungodly" (4:5), "gives life to the death, and calls into being that which is not" (4:17, AT). God promises and performs life from death, salvation from sin, and creation from nothing. Paul is sure that the word of God had not failed, was not failing, and would not fail, because the word of God, from and beyond the beginning, promises and performs the impossible.

Paul is sure that the word of God had not failed, was not failing, and would not fail, because the word of God, from and beyond the beginning, promises and performs the impossible.

Isaac is, in the words of Romans 9:8, a child born by the promise. Romans 4 underlines the impossibility: the age and barrenness of Abraham and Sarah were a death out of which God promised and gave life. It is this creative and out-of-the-opposite word that Paul insists has not and cannot fail. Genealogy does not determine the operation of God's grace: Isaac is a child of God "not according to the flesh, but by the promise." Moving to the next generation in Romans 9:10–13, God's calling of the children of Isaac and Rebekah—Esau and Jacob—also follows this paradoxical but full-of-promise pattern: "And not only so, but also when Rebekah had conceived children by one man, our forefather Isaac, though they were not yet born and had done nothing either good or bad—in order that God's purpose of election might continue, not because of works but because of him who calls—she was told, 'The older will serve the younger.'"

God did not choose Abraham because he was godly; God justified the ungodly. Isaac is not a child of God based on his genealogy; he is born by the promise. Jacob is not chosen because of social status or ethical achievement; God chose the younger before either twin had done anything good or bad. Nothing, it seems, not pedigree or past or performance or potential, is a precondition for God's promise. Romans 9:15–16 parades just this point: "'I will have mercy on whom I have mercy, and I will have compassion on whom I have compassion.' It does not, therefore, depend on human desire or effort, but on God's mercy" (AT). Those opening words are spoken by God in Exodus in the aftermath of Israel's golden calf idolatry. Without regard to human metrics of prestige or value, in the absence of worth and at the moment of need, God has mercy.

This mercy of God that promises the impossible is also what Paul announces God is doing in the present. As Paul proclaims what he calls "the word of Christ" (10:17), God is calling not only Jews but also gentiles (9:24). To name and trace this surprise, Paul quotes from the prophet Hosea: "I will call them 'my people' who are not my people; and I will call her 'my loved one' who is not my loved one," and "In the very place where it was said to them, 'You are not my people,' there they will be called 'children of the living God'" (9:25–26, AT). Each phrase follows the creative and incongruous pattern of God's gracious promise. It is the "not my people" who are called "my people" and "children of the living God"; it is the "not loved" who are called "my loved ones."

The present, however, is also the time of Paul's pain. The grace that calls into being the gentiles as God's people is, at the same time, reducing Israel to a remnant. As Paul laments with words from Isaiah, "Though the number of the sons of Israel be as the sand of the sea, only a remnant of them will be saved" (9:27). In rejecting Jesus, many in Israel have "stumbled over the stumbling stone" (9:32), causing Paul to cry, "My heart's desire and prayer to God for them is that they may be saved" (10:1). According to Paul, "there is no distinction between Jew and Greek" (10:12) at the fundamental level of need and hope: "all have sinned" (3:23) and "all who call on the name of the Lord will be saved" (10:13, AT). As Romans 10 ends, Paul echoes Isaiah's image of God's outstretched hand (10:21). God's word has not failed (9:6), which means the answer to Paul's next question is just as emphatic as his response to the one that opened Romans 9: "Has God rejected his people? No!" (11:1, AT).

Part of Paul's no is that, like Paul, some in Israel do "confess with [their] mouth that Jesus is Lord and believe in [their] heart that God raised him from the dead" (10:9; 11:1–6). Paul's hope, however, has a broader horizon: "all Israel will be saved," and God will "have mercy on all" (11:26, 32). This promise is anchored in God's grace in the past and the present. In the past, with Abraham and Isaac and the exodus, God has called forth life from death and freedom from bondage. In the present, with the gentiles, God is calling "not my people" by the name "my people," and "the not loved" are called "my loved ones." This pattern of grace that, incongruously, is given at the site of sin, bondage, nothing, and death and that, impossibly, gives righteousness, freedom, reality, and life is the shape and source of Paul's hope. Israel has "stumbled" (11:11), "natural branches" have been broken off the "olive tree" that is God's people (11:17–24), but this disobedience and condition of death do not place Israel beyond the range of God's promise and grace. As Paul insists, "the gifts and the calling of God are irrevocable" (11:29), and the grace of this God is always "life from the dead" (11:15) and the promise that does the impossible:

> "this will be my covenant with them
> when I take away their sins." (11:27)

This pattern, according to Paul, is the rhyme scheme of history. Abraham was dead in his trespasses and sins, yet God called him righteous. Abraham's body was dead and Sarah's womb was dead, yet God called Isaac into existence. Jacob had done nothing and did not even exist yet, but God chose to bless him. Israel's disobedience took them to the point of death, yet God's mercy called them into covenant and existence. Through the preaching of the gospel, gentiles, who were not God's people and not loved, are called God's people and named beloved. And on the horizon, as hope and promise and mystery, Israel, though stumbling and dead, will be restored and resurrected by "the deliverer" (11:26). To quote Paul's own summary, "God imprisoned all in disobedience, that he might have mercy on all" (11:32, AT). In the past, the present, and the future, God's word unveils a persistent and perennial need that makes redemption humanly impossible. But just there, at the point of impossibility, God promises and performs that which cannot be but, in Christ, is: freedom and forgiveness, life and being loved. Hearing this promise and announcing this hope, Paul's words turn into worship:

> Oh, the depth and the riches and the wisdom of the knowledge of God! How unsearchable his judgments and his paths beyond tracing out! "Who has known the mind of the Lord? Or who has been his counselor?" "Who has ever given to God that God should repay them?" For from him and through him, and for him are all things. To him be the glory forever and ever! Amen. (11:33–36)

Romans 12–16

This anthem could be a conclusion, but Romans is concrete: this is a letter to "those who are in Rome." Romans 16 displays this on-the-ground, relationally real dynamic with commendations and greetings by name. There is "Phoebe, a deacon of the church," and "Prisca and Aquila," who are "fellow workers in Christ Jesus" (16:1–3). Paul names Epaenetus, Julia, Mary, Persis, Urbanus, and Rufus. Andronicus and Junia are identified as "well known among the apostles" (16:7), and greetings are extended, for example, from Timothy, Tertius, and Erastus (16:21–23). These names specify particular people, with their distinct and real inheritances and histories. The "all" of Romans 11:32—God will have mercy on all—is not an abstraction; "all" means each; it identifies and names the "you" and "us" and "me" in the gospel's promise: Christ died for you, for us, for me. For Paul, this concrete togetherness of distinct but not finally divided people is the communal embodiment of God's promise and grace.

> Christ became a servant to the circumcised to show God's truthfulness, in order to confirm the promises given to the patriarchs, and in order that the Gentiles might glorify God for his mercy. As it is written,
>
> > "Therefore I will praise you among the Gentiles,
> > and sing to your name."
>
> And again it is said,
>
> > "Rejoice, O Gentiles, with his people."
>
> And again,
>
> > "Praise the Lord, all you Gentiles,
> > and let all the peoples extol him."
>
> And again Isaiah says,
>
> > "The root of Jesse will come,
> > even he who arises to rule the Gentiles;
> > in him will the Gentiles hope." (15:8–12)

To return to Romans 3–4, "God is one" and God "will justify the circumcised and the uncircumcised by faith" (3:30, AT), making Abraham "the father of all who believe" (4:11).

Writing "to all those in Rome who are loved by God and called to be saints" (1:7), Paul is addressing an "all" that includes distinct religious and cultural histories. Romans 14, for instance, refers to different principles and practices related to diet and calendar, suggesting disagreement about the continuing significance or requirements of the Jewish law. Paul's basic posture is an inversion of the culturally typical competition for honor. The usual goal, to use the Greek word, was *kleos*: esteem or prestige and its public recording and remembering. Life in the Greco-Roman world could be imagined as a kind of contest—an *agon*—and the comparing and competing had as its finish line a "song-worthy life" (R. N. Goldstein's phrase from *Plato at the Googleplex*). Into this context, and to a community with distinct histories and differing habits, Paul writes, "Outdo one another in showing honor" (12:10). This, for Paul, is the surprising form of freedom and life: "love one another" (12:10). The giving of Christ does not follow the calculus or criteria of worth that cultures and people employ to measure value and build walls between us and them. Christ, given in the absence of worth, creates innovative and boundary-crossing communities that hold together cultural and inherited distinctions that might otherwise divide. Living as "one body" that has "many members" with a range of histories and "gifts that differ" (12:4–6) entails a double pattern of sympathy and solidarity: "let us not pass judgment on one another" but rather relate to each as "the one for whom Christ died" (14:13, 15). This "love," writes Paul, "fulfills the law" (13:8–10).

According to Paul's diagnosis, however, human beings are caught in cycles of worshiping "the creature rather than the Creator" (1:25), of trusting and loving themselves rather than receiving from God and serving their neighbor. At the end of *Freedom of a Christian*, Martin Luther says that the set-free life is described by a double outsideness: "the Christian lives outside her or himself, in God by faith and in the neighbor through love." Under sin, however, the human creature is curved in on the self—*incurvatus in se* (to use the Augustinian image from *City of God*). The question, then, is how God unlocks a person from this prison and pattern of idolatrous self-relation and sets him or her free to relate to God in faith

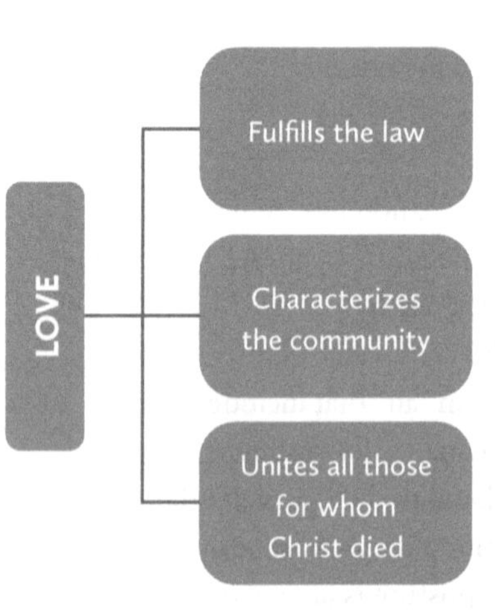

and others in love. If "love fulfills the law," how is love born? (The Beach Boys said their album *Pet Sounds* exists to "increase the love vibe." The question here is how: What creates and increases the "love vibe"?)

The opening of Romans 12 sounds the fundamental note: Paul speaks "by the grace given to me" and makes his "appeal" according to "the mercies of God" (12:3, 1). God's gracious, redeeming love is the source of our grateful, serving love. As 1 John has the headline: "We love because God first loved us." The love that is freedom and law-fulfilling flows from the grace and mercy of God.

Paul's realism about human conflictedness and limitation, reflected so powerfully in Romans 7, for instance, entails a recognition that the invitation to "love one another" does not, in itself, have the power to engender the love it demands and describes. If love fulfills the law (Rom. 13:10) and yet the law cannot "give life" (Gal. 3), then the call to love is not the creation of love.

"The only thing that counts is faith expressing itself through love" (Gal. 5:6).

Romans 5:5 indicates that "God's love for us is poured into our hearts by the Holy Spirit" (AT). This is the "God first loved us," the prior and poured-out love that produces our subsequent and other-serving love. Tracing this movement backward, Paul locates a bridge from "God is love" to "love one another." Galatians 5:6 identifies faith as the font of love: "the only thing that counts is faith expressing itself through love" (AT). Faith as the binding of God's love and ours might not seem immediately apparent, but a consideration of the source of faith uncovers the way it is, in Martin Luther's words, the "cement" that connects us to Christ (*Lectures on Galatians*).

According to Paul, faith, like love, is not generated either by human potential or by divine imperative. "Faith," rather, "comes by hearing, and hearing by the word of Christ" (Rom. 10:17, AT). It is this "word of Christ"—the promise Paul refers to as "the good news" or "gospel" in Romans 10:15—that creates faith. The promise announces God's love; faith is created by and clings to this love; the faith that is being loved by God lives outward and opened up as grateful love to God and serving love for others. As Thomas Cranmer wrote to Henry VIII in 1538, "If the profession of our faith of the remission of our own sins enter within us into the deepness of our hearts, then it must kindle a warm fire of love in our hearts towards God, and towards all others for the love of God" (Annotations to *Institution of a Christian Man*).

After following this pattern in reverse, it is possible to return to the beginning, which is also and always the end: God's love for us in the gospel of Jesus Christ. The summary is: word, faith, love—the word of Christ creates the faith that clings to it, and this faith is active in love. The word of God, however, is two works of God: diagnosis and deliverance, honesty and hope, the revelation of human need for Jesus and the grace of God in the gospel that gives Jesus. This double reality uncovers something of the deep mystery and mercy of God's love-creating love. The God who speaks to us first finds us "in Adam" and "under sin" (Rom. 5–6), locked in our patterns of worshiping the creature rather than the Creator (Rom. 1), and so turned in on ourselves. What God first finds, however, is not who God finally creates: God's love unlocks us as it re-creates us "in Christ" and "under grace" (Rom. 5–6). God's first address to those in Adam occasions the cry, "Who will deliver me?" (7:24). God's final address that crucifies and resurrects us with Christ is, "There is therefore now no condemnation for those who are in Christ Jesus" (8:1). If the diagnosis is that all are "dead in the trespasses and sin," the deliverance is that "God, being rich in mercy, because of the great love with which he loved us, even when we were dead in our trespasses, made us alive together with Christ" (Eph. 2:1–5).

This combined word of honesty and hope lives and loves at the heart of human fear and desire. As the theologian and psychiatrist Frank Lake once wrote, "We oscillate between a desire" to be understood "by communicating and a desire to defend by silence and

secret withdrawal, with the tacit assumption that to leap over the boundaries of reserve, so as to be inwardly known by another person, would be too painful to bear" (*Clinical Theology*). A deep part of the puzzle and pain of human living is that our longing to be understood and loved is often buried under a fear that if we were seen, the other would not stay. The form of life, under this fear, is "masquerade, paper faces on parade" (Webber, *Phantom of the Opera*). Hiding rather than honesty, secrets and shame rather than being seen: as the novelist George Eliot put it, "Our daily familiar life is but a hiding of ourselves from each other" (*Janet's Repentance*). Trapped in this habit of hiding, any "I love you" fears a footnote: the *you* that is loved is not actually *you* but only the mask you present, what the comedian Chris Rock calls "our representatives"; the image we show to the world while under the surface hides a lonely, longing, yet still unseen someone.

But, to quote a prayer, "Almighty God, to whom all hearts are open, all desires known, and from whom no secrets are hid . . ." (Collect for Purity, Book of Common Prayer). As Psalm 139:1 says, "O LORD, you have searched me and known me." The God who speaks sees and knows and understands. The word of God that diagnoses and unearths human need is honesty evoking: it surfaces and names the hurt and need we often feel but cannot face. God takes off the mask and washes off the makeup. God sees and speaks to you. And it is just here—at the site of seen need and understood pain—that God announces the gospel: "while we were still sinners, Christ died for us" (Rom. 5:8). Finally looked upon, we are forever loved. In the words of Walker Percy, God's word is a funeral sermon that says, "I love you dead" (*Love in the Ruins*). But God's graveside speech rolls away the stone: "Wake up, sleeper, rise from the dead and Christ will shine on you" (Eph. 5:14, AT).

This is the "word of Christ"—God's final and forgiving "I love you" spoken in Christ and said to the seen—that creates the faith that is active in love. In the gospel, God says, "I know you and I love you." Faith hears this word; it is being loved by God, and so is given and receives the reality that "I am loved." Love, finally, flows from being loved: word—faith—love.

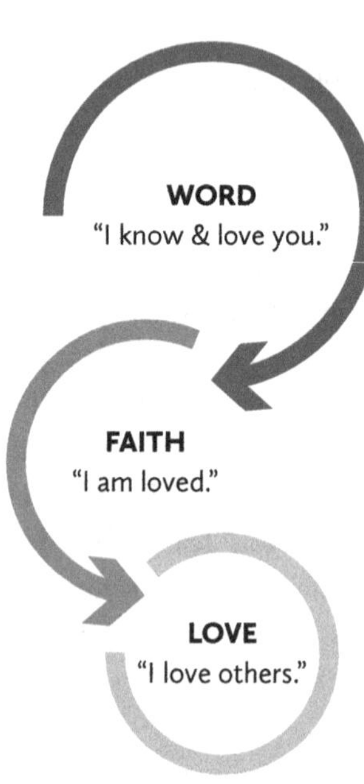

Paul's Pattern for Faith and Life

In Romans, this love of God in the gospel is the first and final word. Both Romans 1:1 and Romans 16:25–27 refer to the "gospel," the "good news about God's Son" who embodies and expresses God's love in this: "while we were still sinners, Christ died for us" (5:8). This is the love with which "God first loved us," the love that both understands and absolves—that sees and stays, that knows and forgives. This is the love that is first; it is also the love that is forever: "nothing in all creation will be able to separate us from the love of God in Christ Jesus" (8:39, AT).

PART 4

Ministers of the Word

CHAPTER 8

Comfortable Words

THE HOLY COMMUNION SERVICE of the Book of Common Prayer includes an invitation that can serve as this final chapter's introduction:

> Hear what comfortable words our Lord Jesus Christ says:
>
> "Come unto me all you who are weary and heavy-laden and I will give you rest" (Matt. 11:28).
>
> "God so loved the world that he gave his only Son so that all who believe in him might not perish, but have everlasting life" (John 3:16).
>
> Hear also what St. Paul says:
>
> "This is a trustworthy saying: Christ Jesus came into the world to save sinners" (1 Tim. 1:15).
>
> Hear also what St. John says:

> "If anyone sin, we have an advocate with the Father, Jesus Christ the righteous, and he is the atoning sacrifice for our sins" (1 John 2:1–2).
>
> Book of Common Prayer (1552)

—

"Can you give me any comfort—any hope?" These words are the final, desperate, honest question of Janet Dempster in George Eliot's short novel *Janet's Repentance.* Janet is trapped in a marriage haunted by spirals of alcoholism and abuse, and her existence is a "weary life to be lived from day to day, with no hope." As Eliot paints the pain, Janet is "crushed," has "nothing to rest on"; "everywhere" seems to be "the same sadness." "Weary and hopeless," Janet remembers a history of "barren exhortation—Do right, and keep a clear conscience, and God will reward you, and your troubles will be easier to bear." But the "path behind her" was "all strewn with broken resolutions," and these exhortations are nothing but "feeble words." It is at this moment of unhidden and bedrock need that Janet poses her question. "While slow difficult tears gathered in her aching eyes," Janet whispered to a minister named Mr. Tryan: "I want to tell you how unhappy I am. . . . I feel no strength to live or die. . . . Can you give me any comfort—any hope?"

This is the first and final question of ministry: At the site of real human sorrow and need, are we left with only "feeble words," or are we given to minister what Thomas Cranmer calls "the comfortable words" (Book of Common Prayer)?

This is also the first and final question of this chapter. Having opened by asking it, the conclusion hopes to address it. In this context, however, the question can be focused: Can ministers of the word give any comfort—any hope? Is "the word of the cross" (1 Cor. 1:18)—"the word of Christ" (Rom. 10:17)—a feeble or a comfortable word? When the question is asked in this way, the path toward it runs through reading and ministering the living and active word of God. This chapter will first consider the nature and pattern of reading Holy Scripture and then move toward the horizon of pastoral care and proclamation—toward the listening and the announcement that honestly hears and addresses Janet's question: in Mr. Tyran's words, "There is comfort, there is hope."

—

The invitation to open Holy Scripture sometimes comes with a flood of plans and prescriptions. Martin Luther once used an image that can simplify. In *On the Councils and the Church,* Luther imagines Scripture as a deep ocean. From that ocean flow many streams: doctrines, devotional habits, patterns of prayer. If we drink from and follow these tributaries upstream and they take us back to and deeper into the source—Holy Scripture—they are streams of "fresh water" that help us hear. Scripture is "breathed out by God" (2 Tim. 3:16), the written form of the "living and active" word (Heb. 4:12) that "goes out from [God's] mouth" and performs God's purpose (Isa. 55:11). Holy Scripture is God speaking. Reading, fundamentally and finally, is hearing, being addressed by and attending to the God who "spoke, and it came to be" (Ps. 33:9). To translate Luther's metaphor, traditions and practices that invite us to open and attend to God's voice are like hearing aids, whereas habits that distract from or muffle the divine address are akin to earplugs.

This is a reminder of the relationship that reading Scripture is. God—the Creator and redeemer—speaks and gives. The reader—the human creature—listens and receives. This relationship is reflected in Psalms. The confession of David in Psalm 51, for instance, is shaped by the revealing and redeeming mercy of God. David "takes" and "lies with" Bathsheba and then, discovering she is pregnant, arranges for the death of her husband, Uriah (2 Sam. 11). The prophet Nathan is given the unenviable task of exposing this sin to the apparently blind and in-denial king. God speaks to David through Nathan, first, to break through the denial and to diagnose his transgression and need.

> And the LORD sent Nathan to David. He came to him and said to him, "There were two men in a certain city, the one rich and the other poor. The rich man had very many flocks and herds, but the poor man had nothing but one little ewe lamb, which he had bought. And he brought it up, and it grew up with him and with his children. It used to eat of his morsel and drink from his cup and lie in his arms, and it was like a daughter to him. Now there came a traveler to the rich man, and he was unwilling to take one of his own flock or herd to prepare for the guest who had come to him, but he took the poor man's lamb and prepared it for the man who had come to him." (2 Sam. 12:1–4)

This parable is initially indirect, but David's reaction indicates that God's word in the form of Nathan's story is digging toward a diagnosis: "[David] said to Nathan, 'As the LORD lives, the man who has done this deserves to die'" (12:5). Then comes what comedians might call the "turn"—the direct word to David: "You are the man" (12:7). God's word performs God's purpose as denial turns to confession: "David said to Nathan, 'I have sinned against the LORD'" (12:13).

It is this honesty, worked by God's word, that is given voice in Psalm 51:

> I know my transgressions,
> and my sin is ever before me. (51:3)

This revelation, however, is not the end of the relationship. Nathan's "word of the LORD" in response to David's "I have sinned" is a merciful surprise: "The LORD also has put away your sin" (2 Sam. 12:13). In Psalm 51, this is expressed as prayer and praise:

> Have mercy on me, O God,
> according to your steadfast love (51:1),

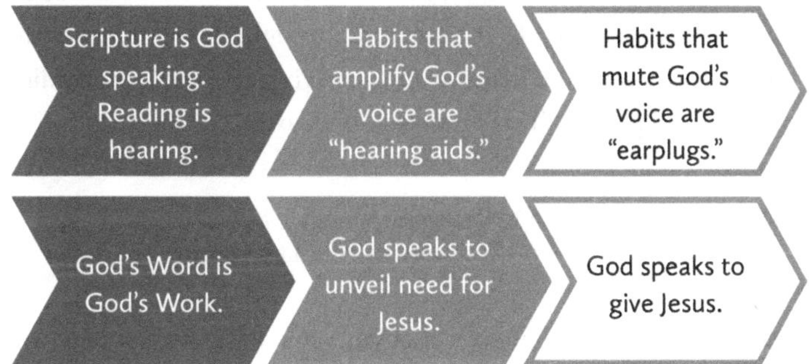

Hearing the Living and Active Word of God

"let the bones that you have broken rejoice" as you "blot out all my iniquities" (51:8–9), and

> my tongue will sing aloud of your righteousness . . .
> and my mouth will declare your praise. (51:14–15)

To quote Psalm 33:9 once more, God "spoke, and it came to be." God's word worked honesty and hope, revealing bondage and need as it set free and forgave. The relationship that reading Scripture is, in other words, the relation we have as hearers and receivers to the speaking and giving God, is the undergoing of God's honesty-engendering and hope-creating address: God unveils our need for Jesus; God gives us Jesus.

This relationship with God in the form of reading Scripture is both celebrated and reflected in Psalm 119. The entire psalm is an extended acrostic extolling the word—statutes, commandments, law, precept, testimonies—of the Lord. Within this psalm, however, the poet is not a lonely reader but is in a living relationship. The fundamental aspect of this is listening, attending to God's address: "I have stored up your word in my heart" (119:11), "I will meditate on your precepts" and "on your wondrous works" (119:15, 27). This is a relationship, however, and the reader "in Psalm 119 is "also a speaker. God's relation to the creature through the word makes the human response-able: hearing and receiving and then responding in praise and prayer: "I will praise you" (119:7),

> Open my eyes, that I may behold
> wondrous things out of your law (119:18),

"teach me, O LORD" (119:33), "Let your steadfast love come to me, O LORD" (119:41). Listening and speaking, receiving and responding, reading and prayer—*meditatio* and *oratio*: this is Creator and creature in communion, in conversation. In Psalm 119, this relationship that is reading and prayer takes place in reality—in the confusion and pain, the fears and suffering of human life.

> If your law had not been my delight,
> I would have perished from my affliction. (119:92)

> I have suffered much.
> Preserve my life, LORD, according to your Word.
> (119:107, AT)

The psalms do not press pause on life; life, rather, pushes the psalmists to honest prayer and urgent study. Experiences of suffering, patterns of failure, questions about God's presence, faithfulness, and forgiveness are the lived context of the communion between the hurting and bound human and the healing and delivering God. Life in relation to God, according to Psalm 119, is listening and prayer in the context of real life: *meditatio*, *oratio*, and *tentatio*. That last word, *tentatio*, means something like suffering or spiritual attack, and it is a reminder that God relates to real rather than fictional people. Sorrow and shame, sin and suffering, confusion and death occasion cries such as, "My soul clings to the dust" (119:25). It is just here, however, at the open wound of honest need, asking if God does or

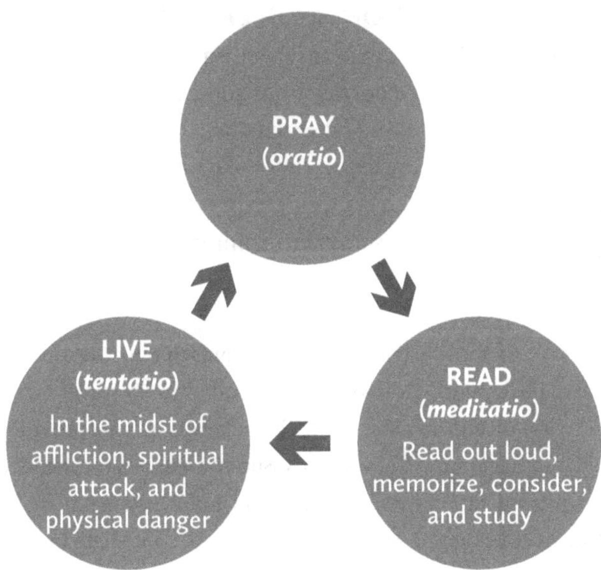

Pattern of Psalm 119

ever could love *me*, that the promise sounds again: "God's word," sings the psalmist, "is my comfort in my affliction, . . . your promise gives me life" (119:49–50).

This moves us closer to Janet's question. "Is there any comfort?" she asks. "Your word," answers Psalm 119, "is my comfort." If the church is a "creature of the word," and preaching and pastoral care are "ministries of the word," Psalm 119 would suggest that these are the site and the speaking of "comfortable words." For many, however, "church" and "sermon" are words that are fearful as well as "feeble." In a novel by William Inge, a suffering and ashamed mother says to her son, "Church isn't a place you can go to with your troubles. Church is just a place you go when things are going well and you have a new hat to wear." As the author then comments, in a line pregnant with his own experience, "There was a little bitterness in what she said. . . . But there was also truth" (*My*

Son Is a Splendid Driver). Or consider a song about not wanting to hear a sermon. "Daddy, I'm in trouble deep," sings a daughter, and "in times of trouble" (to borrow from another song), a sermon, it seems, would be something other than help or hope: "Papa, Don't Preach" (Madonna). The experiences of pain, condemnation, and shallowness in the face of suffering expressed in these lines pose the question once more: Is there any comfort—any hope? As Mark Rutherford wrote in 1887:

> It is surely a terrible charge to bring against a religious system, that in the conflict which has to be waged by every son of Adam with disease, misfortune, death, the believers in it are provided with neither armour nor weapons. Surely a real religion, handed down from century to century, ought to have accumulated a store of consolatory truths which will be of some help to us in time of need. If it can tell us nothing, if we cannot face a single disaster any the better for it, and if we never dream of turning to it when we are in distress, of what value is it? (*The Revolution in Tanner's Lane*)

The only answers to a question asked from this depth of honesty and hurt are either silence or a divine mercy that sees and understands human need yet also acts to restore and console, to set free and forgive. "A consolation you could believe in," writes Francis Spufford, "would be one that didn't have to be kept apart from awkward areas of reality. One that didn't depend on some more or less tacky fantasy about us, and therefore one that wasn't in danger of popping like a soap bubble upon contact with ordinary truths about us" (*Unapologetic*). This is what Martin Luther was asking after in 1518 in his *Enquiry into Truth for the Consolation of Troubled Consciences*. His hope—his urgent pastoral and personal need—was to understand "the gospel, not only in words but in affections and experience" (*Lectures on Galatians*). "Ideas are often poor ghosts," observes George Eliot, "they pass athwart us in thin vapour, and cannot make themselves felt" (*Janet's Repentance*). Luther's question—our question—is whether the "word of Christ" is a feeble or comfortable word, only a ghost, or actually the gospel.

This question is at the bedrock, close to the bone. But bones, as it happens, name a place and pattern of God's mercy and love. "Let the bones that you have broken rejoice," sings Psalm 51, as honest confession turns to hope:

> Hide your face from my sins,
> and blot out all my iniquities. (51:8–9)

It is in a valley of dry bones that the Lord both poses a question to Ezekiel—"can these bones live?"—and answers it with power and promise: "Thus says the Lord God . . . So I prophesied . . . and they lived. . . . Thus says the Lord God: Behold, I will open your graves" (37:3, 9–14). Not even the grave can reduce God's word to a ghost, because death loses its sting (1 Cor. 15) at the sound of a grace that rolls away the stone. Apart from this "grace of God," Luther recognized, our "bones" are "weary" and get "no rest" (*Lectures on Galatians*). But as another sixteenth-century student of Scripture discovered, "bruised bones" and a "heart" that "was wounded . . . leapt for joy" after hearing the grave-opening gospel from 1 Timothy 1:15: "Christ Jesus came into the world to save sinners" (Thomas Bilney in 1519, recorded in John Foxe's *Actes and Monuments* from 1570).

These images and stories are a reminder: "It is just here," to quote W. H. Auden again, "among the ruins and the bones, that we may rejoice in the perfected work that is not our own" (*The Sea and the Mirror*). God speaks at the site of human need, unearthing the honesty that is "good soil" for the divine word that is planted in an open wound. The divine "I know you" understands, sees, and surfaces the hidden, denied, and buried realities of human living. We are, as Pindar said millennia ago, "creatures of a day" ("Pythian VIII") who nevertheless "desire to stand out," who "ache" for "cosmic specialness" (Ernest Becker, *The Denial of Death*). This, as

Bob Dylan sings, is the "weary tune," the "song we strum" when life feels like a fragile and endless audition for finally being enough—for being loved ("Lay Down Your Weary Tune"). Human existence can feel like an exhausting equation: the value of and verdict on life is the sum of one's pedigree, past, and performance. The human creature is both, in George Herbert's resonant phrase, "sighing to be approved" ("A True Hymne") and overburdened by a feeling and fear that a person's biography cannot finally carry the weight of his or her belovedness.

God's no to righteousness by works of law (see Gal. 2:16; Rom. 3:28) recognizes this impossible and inhuman habit of anchoring life and answering death on the basis of achievement or inheritance. The divine word that diagnoses and unearths the honest, to commandeer a description, is "a truth-teller on the unspeakables of the human condition" (*The Denial of Death*). The primal lie that "you will be like God" and "you will not surely die" (Gen. 3:4–5) is exposed and outvolumed by a true love that sees and says what is: "I am the LORD your God" (Exod. 20:2), and you are "dead in [your] trespasses and sins" (Eph. 2:1). This is the word of the Lord who has "searched me and known me" (Ps. 139:1), the God before whom "all hearts are open, all desires known, and from whom no secrets are hid" (Collect for Purity). In the words of Exodus 3:7, God "sees." But what does God then say? Is there any comfort—any hope?

"Then the LORD said, 'I have surely seen the affliction of my people who are in Egypt and have heard their cry. . . . I know their sufferings, and I have come down to deliver them'" (Exod. 3:7–8). God sees, God hears, God knows. And God has "come down to deliver." The "living and active word is sharper than a two-edged sword" (Heb. 4:12, AT), both cutting through denial and distraction and cutting to the honest human cry: "Who will deliver me?" (Rom. 7:24). This question, prompted by God's diagnosing and revealing truth, is always answered by God's delivering and resurrecting mercy: "while we were still sinners"—seen and heard by God in our bondage and need—"Christ died for us" (Rom. 5:8).

Is there any comfort? "There is therefore now no condemnation for those who are in Christ Jesus" (Rom. 8:1). Is there any hope? "Christ is risen," shouts the Easter anthem, and "nothing in all creation"—"neither death nor life"— can "separate us from the love of God in Christ Jesus our Lord" (Rom. 8:38–39).

At the time Janet asked her question ("any comfort?"), a life of "sorrow" and "broken resolutions" had exposed the hopelessness of "all other hopes"—all hopes, that is, "except his love alone" (*Janet's Repentance*). This "one thing needful" (Luke 10:42) is a diamond thread of mercy even when all else has turned to ash. As Mr. Tryan says to Janet, it is "the helpless who feel themselves helpless that God specially invites. . . . You are weary and heavy-laden; well, it is you Christ invites to come to him and find rest" (*Janet's Repentance*; see Matt. 11:28). Honesty, it seems, is the site of hope. "Christ's name," suggests Martin Luther with an image from Isaiah, is "a bruised reed he will not break," and his pattern is always to meet honest need with redeeming mercy: "he helps the penitent, comforts the afflicted, recalls the despairing, raises up the fallen, justifies sinners, gives life to the dying" (*Lecture on Psalm 45*). In Jesus's own words, the "Spirit is upon me," and the Father "has anointed me to proclaim good news to the poor . . . liberty to the captives and recovering of sight to the blind, freedom to the oppressed, to announce the year of the Lord's forgiveness" (Luke 4:18–19, quoting Isa. 61, AT). God's "I know you" sees at the site of sorrow, aloneness, bondage, sin, and death. God's "I love you"—spoken to *you* with all the personal history and hurt such a pronoun can carry—speaks and gives the one who comforts, adopts, liberates, forgives, and makes alive.

This is the motif of mercy: yesterday, today, and then again "tomorrow and tomorrow and tomorrow" (Shakespeare, *Macbeth*), deep and real need names the when and the for whom of God's grace. "While we were still sinners, Christ died for us" (Rom. 5:8). This pattern of mercy shapes the practice of ministry. God's word is both a double work and a concrete address: it engenders honesty and gives hope by gifting Jesus to *you* (or us or me). The ministry of this word, therefore, is "not . . . idle knowledge" but pastoral presence and proclamation that "uplifts and consoles terrified hearts," that "produces peace" and "joy" and that "consoles in the midst of fears" (Melanchthon, *Apology of the Augsburg Confession,* 1531).

These phrases—"consoles terrified hearts" and "consoles in the midst of fears"—are a reminder that ministry is shaped by "the same old song" (Four Tops): God's word both uncovers and understands suffering and need even as it wipes away every tear, forgives, and forever loves. What ministry names is not a new word but a "bridge over troubled water" (Simon & Garfunkel), a way that the word of the "holy, holy, holy" Lord (Rev. 4:8) makes contact with and finally comforts those who are, in Thornton Wilder's comical yet realistic description, "diseased and dying and deaf and blind and as busy as clowns" (*The Alcestiad*). "God was in Christ, reconciling the world to himself, not counting their trespasses against them" (2 Cor. 5:19, AT). As Martin Luther recognized, however, "because this grace would benefit no one if it remained . . . hidden and could not come to us, the Holy Spirit comes and gives himself to us . . . through the gospel" (*Confession concerning Christ's Supper,* 1528). Or even more emphatically: "The word, the word, the word," Luther shouts in *Against the Heavenly Prophets,* "the word does it. For if Christ had been given and crucified for us a thousand times, it would all be for nothing had not the word of God come and distributed it to us and given it to me as a gift." This strong language is an insistence that the word we minister is no ghost; it is the gospel: the good news about the gift of God's Son for us that, as the Holy Spirit speaks, gives that same Son to us. This can be considered under two headings, borrowing prepositional phrases from the eighteenth-century author J. G. Hamann: ministry is a meeting place where God speaks and is present both "to the creature" and "through the creature" (*Aesthetica in nuce*).

To the creature: ministry engages particular, real people and attends to what God, in the Holy Spirit and through the word, is doing to, with, and for them. "To have someone listen," Taylor Caldwell once wrote, "not as a patient but as a human soul," to be heard "without hurry, without the click of a clock, is the direst need of our spirits" (*The Man Who Listens*). This assertion is an echo: God's word sees, knows, understands, hears. We often live, as Caldwell puts it, as "sealed vessels," behind walls of hidden shame and above layers of buried pasts. The "divine I know you" is often spoken in the silence of pastoral listening. This maps ministry onto the word that unearths honest need and gives hope by giving Jesus. Because God's word is both a double work and a personal address, ministering this word means both discerning the person and distinguishing the word. These are both forms of listening before they become witness.

Three questions: Who? Which? What? The first question—who?—attends to the concreteness of God's presence and promise. With whom is God speaking? What history, questions, hurt, and confusion are surfacing as God sees and understands? Is the person distracted and still denying hidden need, or has God's honesty-engendering word dug through the rubble to the bedrock where each person asks, "Who will deliver me?" This attentive, nondirective, undemanding, "nothing you confess could make me love you less" listening (The Pretenders, "I'll Stand by You") has, in Paul Zahl's words, "the unique potential for getting your pain out," "for digging below the surface to the ancient but hitherto un-accessed buried cave of the worst hurt you ever had" (*Peace in the Last Third of Life*). The second question—which?—is another layer of listening. Which word is God speaking to this person at this time? Is God addressing the "old Adam" who lives according to the ancient lie and needs a diagnosis deeper than this deceit: "I am the Lord your God," and you are "dead in your trespasses and sins"? Or is that tomb sealed, and God is speaking at the graveside to roll away the stone: "you who were dead in your trespasses . . . God made alive together with Christ, having forgiven all your sins" (Col. 2:13, AT). This kind of listening is already an intimation of

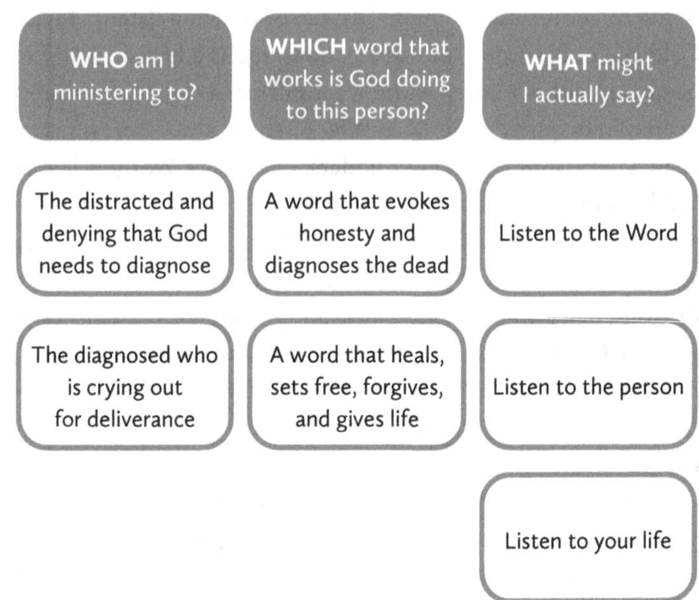

grace. When a person is seen and another person stays, it is the merciful surprise of being beheld and beloved. Fear and judgment are the cocoon in which our often-felt-but-rarely-faced fear and past hides and metamorphosizes into shame. Being listened to, looked at, and still loved, by contrast, is embodied and experienced mercy. Honesty and hope are often translated into pastoral (and personal) relationships as listening and time—attentively and actually being there, patiently and unconditionally staying there.

At this point, having asked the listening questions "who?" and "which?" the third question might follow: What? This is also a listening question, though it has a horizon of proclamation. To ask what words should be unsaid and what words—to this person or people at this moment with this need—might be spoken is to listen: to God's word, to the person, and to your own life. The words that minister God's word that reveals human need can take the form of the Ten Commandments (Exod. 20), questions such as to Adam, "Where are you?" (Gen. 3:9), to Cain, "Where is . . . your brother?"

(Gen. 4:9), Nathan's story about sheep that builds to a turn, "You are the man" (2 Sam. 12:7), or Jesus's delusion-shattering yet loving line, "You lack one thing" (Mark 10:21). This variety is an indication that the human habit of hiding suffering and sin behind a shield-wall of denial, repression, and distraction is met with a diagnosing mercy that breaks through or digs beneath our defenses. This is sometimes direct ("thus says the Lord"), but often the path to the fearful, ashamed, hiding, and hurting person is through an honest description of life, indirect but in-touch parables, humor, and non-self-involved personal vulnerability.

This ministry is a kind of archaeology, an excavation that unearths honesty: "Who will deliver me?" (Rom. 7:24). To "look life in the face," says José Ortega y Gasset, "is to feel oneself lost." The honest are shipwrecked; they "will look round for something to which to cling. . . . These are the only genuine ideas; the ideas of the shipwrecked. All the rest are rhetoric posturing, and farce" (*The Revolt of the Masses*). Is there any comfort—any hope? Is there a word that is genuine or only a ghost? Are we left with farce and feeble words, or is there something to which to cling, a comfortable word? Here, behind the defenses and at the sound of an honest cry for deliverance, God's word is distilled and more declarative: there is "no one else," "no other name" (Acts 4:12). The gospel is and only is, as Paul insists in Galatians, "the gospel of Christ" (Gal. 1:7). As a confused servant of the queen of the Ethiopians read Isaiah, Philip spoke from this Scripture "the good news about Jesus" (Acts 8:26–35). On the road to Emmaus, Jesus announced his suffering and glory in the ruins of the dashed hopes of his followers; "beginning with Moses and all the Prophets, he interpreted to them in all the Scriptures the things concerning himself" (Luke 24:13–27). Among the Corinthians, Paul "determined to know nothing but Christ and him crucified" (1 Cor. 2:2, AT), to declare only this name because "at the name of Jesus every knee [will] bow" (Phil. 2:10) and "all who call on the name of the Lord will be saved" (Rom. 10:13, AT).

This name—Jesus—is "love . . . strong as death" (Song of Sol. 8:6), and it is in this name that uncovered need is met with promised hope: "The LORD has put away your sin; you shall not die" (2 Sam. 12:13); "Thanks be to God through Jesus Christ our Lord. . . . There is therefore now no condemnation for those who are in Christ Jesus" (Rom. 7:25–8:1); "Fear not, I am the first and the last, and the living one. I died, and behold I am alive forevermore" (Rev. 1:17–18). Jesus Christ is, as Paul confesses, "the Son of God, who loved me and gave himself for me" (Gal. 2:20). To minister the gospel today and tomorrow is to proclaim the word that the Holy Spirit speaks to give that same Son to someone Jesus loves and gave himself for. In the words of 2 Corinthians 5:20, "We are ambassadors for Christ, God making his appeal through us." We have what Paul calls "the ministry of reconciliation," speaking the present-tense promise: "Be reconciled to God," because "God was in Christ reconciling the world to himself" (2 Cor. 5:18–20, AT). God's mercies "are new every morning" (Lam. 3:22–23), and each "today" is a new "now is the day of salvation" (2 Cor. 6:2). The promise we proclaim is God's own ancient yet unaging and ever new I-to-you love: "You are my beloved child, with you I am well pleased" (Luke 3:22), "as far as the east is from the west, so far have I removed your sins from you" (Ps. 103:12, AT), "this is my body given—my blood poured out—for you" (Luke 22:19–20, AT).

Through the creature: the mystery—and the mercy—of ministry is that God, in grace, communes with limited yet loved creatures by speaking and giving himself through creatures. "The word became flesh and dwelt among us" (John 1:14). "That which was from the beginning, which we have heard, which we have seen with our eyes, which we looked upon and have touched with our hands, concerning the word of life . . . that which we have seen and heard we proclaim also to you" (1 John 1:1–3). As Athanasius, a fourth-century North African theologian, writes, "By nature" the Creator "is beyond all being," and yet by "love" and "grace" there is a bridge across this "beyondness": "in these last days [God] has spoken to us by his Son," and "in Christ God was reconciling the world to himself" (Heb. 1:1–2 and 2 Cor. 5:19; for Athanasius see *Contra Gentes* and *On the Incarnation*). The language of God's love is the creaturely life and death of Jesus. "In this the love of God was made manifest among us, that God sent his only Son into the world. . . . In this is love, not that we have loved God but that he loved us and sent his Son to be the atoning sacrifice for our sins" (1 John 4:9–10, AT).

The gospel tells the story of and gives this incarnate, crucified, and risen Son. And here God's creaturely communion continues: the embodied Jesus is given to embodied people through bodily words. Holy Scripture is the Holy Spirit speaking through ink on a page; proclamation is divine speech through human mouth to human ears; and baptism and the Lord's Supper preach and promise Jesus Christ as God's word united to water, bread, and wine. "We have this treasure in jars of clay" (2 Cor. 4:7), writes Paul, as "the Father of mercies and God of all comfort" (1:3) has spoken and "shone the glory of God in the face of Jesus Christ" (4:6, AT). When Janet asks Mr. Tryan if there is "any comfort—any hope," she is speaking to "a fellow sinner," one who has "needed the same comfort." His wound, like Paul's "weakness" (2 Cor. 11:30; 12:9–10), gives voice to the "tale of divine pity" as a comfortable rather than a feeble word: because he has "suffered life," Janet realizes, Mr. Tryan's words touch her own pain like "rain failing on the parched earth" (Eliot, *Janet's Repentance*).

This "through the creature" mercy is the theme of a short but profound play by Thornton Wilder entitled *The Angel That Troubled the Waters.* At the pool of Bethesda (à la John 5), an angel addresses a man who is hurting but is also a source of healing: "Without your wound where would your power be? It is your very remorse that makes your low voice tremble into the hearts of men. The very angels themselves cannot persuade the wretched and blundering children on earth as can one human being broken on the wheel of living. In Love's service only wounded soldiers can serve." As the Holy Spirit gives Jesus in the gospel, the "jars of clay" through whom

God speaks are, in solidarity and sympathy with those to whom God speaks, weak and unworthy (Rom. 5:6–10 and Rev. 5:3–4), "fellow sinners" who have "needed the same comfort." In Paul's words, God's "power is made perfect in weakness" (2 Cor. 12:9). In Wilder's echo, "In Love's service only wounded soldiers can serve."

In Love's service, however, wounded soldiers do, finally, have something to say. To quote Mr. Tryan one last time, "There is comfort, there is hope. . . . I speak from my own deep and hard experience" (Eliot, *Janet's Repentance*). Remember Revelation 5: The "Lord God Almighty" is on the throne holding a scroll, "and no one in heaven or on earth or under the earth was able to open the scroll or to look into it." As he sees this, John says, "I began to weep loudly because no one was found worthy to open the scroll." Unworthy and weeping: reality and honest need have been unveiled. But then comes a comfortable word, spoken to the weeping by another of the unworthy: "Weep no more; behold, the Lion of the tribe of Judah, the Root of David, has conquered." John looks, and through tear-filled eyes, behold: "a Lamb standing, as though it had been slain" (Rev. 5:1–6). In Paul's words, "What we proclaim is not ourselves, but Jesus Christ as Lord" (2 Cor. 4:5). "The hope that is within you" (1 Pet. 3:15) is the hope you have heard; it is what you have to give because it is, by grace, what you have been given (1 Cor. 4:7). There is "no other name" (Acts 4:12), no "other gospel" (Gal. 1:6). There is only "the name above every name" (Phil. 2:9), the one "gospel of Christ" (Gal. 1:7). This gospel, as Oswald Bayer writes, "must always be spoken anew . . . for the only thing we can say new is what will never again become old" ("Preaching the Word"). In Paul's Easter announcement, "Christ, being raised from the dead, will never die again" (Rom. 6:9). With death defeated, the gospel of "the living one"—the one who says, "I died, and behold I am alive forevermore"—is ever new and always today's news (Rev. 1:18). To those who are afraid and exhausted by living as if life was an endless and always failing audition for love, the gospel says, "God so loved, he gave" (John 3:16). To those who, as Hebrews has it, have lived in "slavery to the fear of death," the Easter anthem sings of grace that opens the grave:

> "O death, where is your victory?
> O death, where is your sting?" (1 Cor. 15:55)

And to those who are breaking under the burden of attempting to carry the weight of their own worth, the comfortable word lifts the burden as it is carried by the one who said, "Come unto to me all you who are weary and heavy-laden and I will give you rest" (Matt. 11:28, AT).

This is no ghost; this is the gospel: at the site of sorrow, sin, bondage, and death, Jesus comes to wipe away tears, forgive, set free, and make alive. Ministry is not an exemption from the universal league of the unworthy. Rather, in solidarity and sympathy, ministry means listening and listening and ultimately joining the chorus that sings, "What we proclaim is not ourselves, but Jesus Christ as Lord" (2 Cor. 4:5); "weep no more; behold the Lion of the tribe of Judah" (Rev. 5:5); "behold, the Lamb of God, who takes away the sin of the world" (John 1:29, 36). Beholding that lamb, we see "the glory of God in the face of Jesus Christ" (2 Cor. 4:6) and the "love God shows in this way: while we were still sinners, Christ died for us" (Rom. 5:8, AT). This is the final and forever word: "It is finished" (John 19:30), and "neither death nor life . . . nor anything else in all creation, will be able to separate us from the love of God in Christ Jesus" (Rom. 8:38–39). Jesus is, as Galatians 4 proclaims, the Son of God who, by grace, makes us sons and daughters of God. "Worthy is the Lamb who was slain" (Rev. 5:12), for in him what the Father has always said to the eternal Son, God, by grace, is forever and finally saying to you: "You are my beloved child, in you I am well pleased."

Acknowledgments

THIS BOOK BEGAN AS A SERIES of lectures delivered to Olympians who were training to be chaplains with the United States Council for Sports Chaplaincy (USCSC). I was invited to offer an introduction to and overview of Holy Scripture, a case study and theological synthesis of Paul's letter to the Romans, and a reflection on reading and ministering the word. That focus and scope remain the content and shape of this book. The presentation of the material does not presume (or, I hope, require) university or divinity school theological education. Most critical matters of, for example, composition and context are left unexplored, and the many studies and scholars who have informed my presentation and understanding are mostly unnamed. The constraints of space also mean that this canonical exploration is an overview with representative exegetical samples rather than a comprehensive survey of the Old and New Testaments. The hope is to provide an introduction that functions as an invitation: take up and read Holy Scripture.

The informal, spoken style of that initial lecture setting has been retained, but that should not disguise the editorial effort needed to transpose the words from lecture to manuscript. For that I am especially grateful to Alysia Yates for her time, care, and help. For the further move from transposed lectures to translation into a book, I am glad to express my gratitude to my research assistant and doctoral student, Laura Henrich, who assisted significantly with the final editing and preparation of the manuscript. Orrey McFarland provided an insightful peer-review, and the book is both more precise and more pastoral because of him. My colleagues, Mark Gignilliat, Chip Hardy, and Alex Kirk, each read one of the chapters on the Old Testament, and that section is the better because of their expertise and generosity. I'm also grateful for Wesley Hill, Gerald Bray, Gil Kracke, and—as always and with all I write—Megan Linebaugh, who read through the entire book with care and insight.

And a particular pleasure: thank you, Callie (one of my daughters), for your help typing and editing part of this book—you're far better at both than I will ever be!

I am also grateful to those who invited me to deliver these lectures (Madeline Manning Mims and Ashley Null) and especially to those who came to learn: the Olympians who are students of Holy Scripture for the sake of proclaiming the good news of God's mercy in Jesus in and for a competitive and weary world.

This book is dedicated to those first USCSC students, and also to my brother, Josh, an Olympic-caliber athlete who kept asking for a book more like this.

Further Reading

INTRODUCTION: THE STORY AND SHAPE OF HOLY SCRIPTURE

Kleinig, John W. *God's Word: A Guide to Holy Scripture*. Lexham, 2022.

CHAPTER 1: LAW (TORAH)

Gignilliat, Mark, and Heath Thomas. *Reading the Old Testament as Christian Scripture*. Baker Academic, 2025.

Wenham, Gordon. *Exploring the Old Testament: A Guide to the Pentateuch*. InterVarsity Press, 2003.

CHAPTER 2: THE PROPHETS (NEVI'IM)

Arterbury, E. A., W. H. Bellinger Jr., and D. S. Dodson. *Engaging the Christian Scriptures: An Introduction to the Bible*. Baker Academic, 2014.

CHAPTER 3: THE WRITINGS (KETUVIM)

Davis, Ellen. *Getting Involved with God: Rediscovering the Old Testament*. Cowley, 2001.

———. *Opening Israel's Scriptures*. Oxford University Press, 2019.

CHAPTER 4: THE GOSPELS

Bauckham, Richard. *Jesus: A Very Short Introduction*. Oxford University Press, 2011.

CHAPTER 5: THE LETTERS (AND LIFE) OF PAUL

Barclay, John M. G. *Paul and the Power of Grace*. Eerdmans, 2020.
Linebaugh, Jonathan A. *The Word of the Cross: Reading Paul*. Eerdmans, 2022.

CHAPTER 6: HEBREWS TO REVELATION

Campbell, C. R., and J. T. Pennington. *Reading the New Testament as Christian Scripture: A Literary, Canonical, and Theological Survey*. Baker Academic, 2020.

CHAPTERS 7: PAUL'S LETTER TO THE ROMANS

Gaventa, Beverly Roberts. *When in Romans: An Invitation to Linger with the Gospel according to Paul*. Baker Academic, 2016.
Westerholm, Stephen. *Preface to the Study of Paul*. Eerdmans, 1997.

CHAPTER 8: COMFORTABLE WORDS

Gerhard, Johann. *Handbook of Consolations*. 1611. Wipf & Stock, 2009.
Senkbeil, Harold L. *The Care of Souls: Cultivating a Pastor's Heart*. Lexham, 2019.

Bibliography

Arterbury, E. A., W. H. Bellinger Jr., and D. S. Dodson. *Engaging the Christian Scriptures: An Introduction to the Bible*. Grand Rapids: Baker Academic, 2014.

Athanasius. *Contra Gentes and De Incarnatione*. Edited by R. W. Thomson. In *Oxford Early Christian Texts*. Oxford: Oxford University Press, 1971.

———. *On the Incarnation*. Translated and edited by A Religious of C.S.M.V. Crestwood, NY: St. Vladimir's Seminary Press, 2003.

Auden, W. H. *For the Time Being: A Christmas Oratorio*. Edited by Alan Jacobs. Princeton: Princeton University Press, 2013.

———. *The Sea and the Mirror: A Commentary on Shakespeare's* The Tempest. Edited by Arthur C. Kirsch. Princeton: Princeton University Press, 2005.

———. *The Shield of Achilles*. Edited by Alan Jacobs. Princeton: Princeton University Press, 2024.

Augustine. *City of God*. Translated by Henry Bettenson. New York: Penguin Classics, 2003.

———. *Confessions*. Translated by Henry Chadwick. New York: Oxford University Press, 1991.

———. *Enarrationes in Psalmos*. Edited by G. Franco. Corpus Scriptorum Ecclesiasticorum Latinorum. Vienna: Austrian Academy of Sciences Press, 2011.

———. *On Christian Teaching*. Translated by R. P. H. Green. New York: Oxford University Press, 2008.

Barclay, John M. G. *Paul and the Power of Grace*. Grand Rapids: Eerdmans, 2020.

Bauckham, Richard. *Jesus: A Very Short Introduction*. New York: Oxford University Press, 2011.

Bayer, Oswald. "Preaching the Word." In *Justification Is for Preaching*. Edited by Virgil Thompson. Eugene, OR: Pickwick, 2012.

The Beach Boys. *Pet Sounds*. Capitol Records, 1966.

Becker, Ernest. *The Denial of Death*. New York: Free Press, 1973.

Bilney, Thomas. 1518. Recorded in John Foxe's *Actes and Monuments*. Edited by S. R. Cattley. London: Seely & Burnside, 1837 (1563).

Bonhoeffer, Dietrich. *Letters and Papers from Prison*. Edited by Eberhard Bethge. New York: Simon & Schuster, 1997.

Book of Common Prayer. 1552. In *The First and Second Prayer-Books of King Edward the Sixth*. London: J. M. Dent & Sons, 1910.

Caldwell, Taylor. *The Man Who Listens*. London: Collins, 1961.

Campbell, C. R., and J. T. Pennington. *Reading the New Testament as Christian Scripture: A Literary, Canonical, and Theological Survey*. Grand Rapids: Baker Academic, 2020.

Cash, Johnny. "The Fourth Man." *The Holy Land*, 1969.

Cervantes, Miguel de. *Don Quixote*. Translated by P. A. Motteaux. Ware, England: Wordsworth Editions, 1993.

Cranach, Lucas. *Law and Gospel*. 1530. Woodcut. In *German Engravings, Etchings, and Woodcuts, c. 1400–1700*. Compiled by F. W. H. Hollstein. Amsterdam, 1954.

———. *Martin Luther Preaching* (or *Reformation Altarpiece*). 1547. Oil on wood. Evangelische Stadtkirche St. Marien, Wittenberg.

Cranmer, Thomas. Annotations to Henry VIII Corrections to *Institution of a Christian Man*. In J. E. Cox, *Miscellaneous Writings and Letters of Thomas Cranmer*. Cambridge: Parker Society, 1846.

Davis, Ellen. *Getting Involved with God: Rediscovering the Old Testament*. Lanham, MD: Cowley, 2001.

———. *Opening Israel's Scriptures*. Oxford: Oxford University Press, 2019.

Dylan, Bob. "Death Is Not the End." *Down in the Groove*, 1988.

———. "Lay Down Your Weary Tune." 1963. *Biograph* 4, 1985.

Eliot, George. *Janet's Repentance*. 1858. In *Scenes of Clerical Life*. London: Penguin Books, 1985.

Four Tops. "It's the Same Old Song." *Four Tops' Second Album*, 1965.

Gathercole, Simon. *The Gospel and the Gospels: Christian Proclamation and Early Jesus Books*. Grand Rapids: Eerdmans, 2022.

Gaventa, Beverly Roberts. *When in Romans: An Invitation to Linger with the Gospel according to Paul*. Grand Rapids: Baker Academic, 2016.

Gerhard, Johann. *Handbook of Consolations*. 1611. Eugene, OR: Wipf & Stock, 2009.

Gignilliat, Mark, and Heath Thomas. *Reading the Old Testament as Christian Scripture*. Grand Rapids: Baker Academic, 2025.

Goldstein, R. N. *Plato at the Googleplex: Why Philosophy Won't Go Away*. New York: Pantheon, 2014.

Grünewald, Matthias. "John the Baptist." From the *Isenheim Altarpiece*. Oil on Panel. 1510–1515.

Hamann, J. G. *Aesthetica in nuce: A Rhapsody in Cabbalistic Prose*. 1762. In *Writings on Philosophy and Language*. Edited by K. Haynes. Cambridge: Cambridge University Press, 2007.

The Heidelberg Catechism. In *Creeds, Confessions, and Catechisms: A Reader's Edition*. Edited by Chad Van Dixhoorn. Wheaton, IL: Crossway, 2022.

Henze, Matthias. *4 Ezra and 2 Baruch: Translations, Introductions, and Notes*. Minneapolis: Fortress, 2013.

Herbert, George. "Holy Scripture I." In *The Temple: Sacred Poems and Private Ejaculations*. London, 1633.

———. "A True Hymne." In *The Temple: Sacred Poems and Private Ejaculations*. London, 1633.

Inge, William. *My Son Is a Splendid Driver*. Boston: Little, Brown, 1971.

Jenson, Robert W. *A Theology in Outline: Can These Bones Live?* Edited by Adam Eitel. New York: Oxford University Press, 2016.

Johnson, Samuel. "Know Thyself." 1772. In *Samuel Johnson: The Ma-*

jor Works. Edited by D. Greene. New York: Oxford University Press, 2009.

———. "The Vanity of Human Wishes." 1749. In *Samuel Johnson: The Major Works*. Edited by D. Greene. New York: Oxford University Press, 2009.

Käsemann, Ernst. *An die Römer*. Handbuch zum Neuen Testament 8a. Tübingen: Mohr Siebeck, 1973.

———. *Commentary on Romans*. Translated by G. W. Bromiley. Grand Rapids: Eerdmans, 1980.

Kleinig, John W. *God's Word: A Guide to Holy Scripture*. Bellingham, WA: Lexham, 2022.

Lake, Frank. *Clinical Theology: A Theological and Psychiatric Basis to Clinical Pastoral Care*. 2 vols. Jackson, GA: Emeth, 2006 (1966).

Linebaugh, Jonathan. *The Word of the Cross: Reading Paul*. Grand Rapids: Eerdmans, 2022.

Lloyd-Jones, Sally. *The Jesus Storybook Bible: Every Story Whispers His Name*. Grand Rapids: Zondervan, 2007.

Luther, Martin. *Against the Heavenly Prophets in the Matter of Images and Sacraments*. 1525. In *Luther's Works*. American ed. Philadelphia: Fortress; St. Louis: Concordia, 1955–.

———. *A Brief Instruction on What to Look for and Expect in the Gospels*. 1521. In *Luther's Works*. American ed. Philadelphia: Fortress; St. Louis: Concordia, 1955–.

———. *Confession concerning Christ's Supper*. 1528. In *Luther's Works*. American ed. Philadelphia: Fortress; St. Louis: Concordia, 1955–.

———. *Disputation against Scholastic Theology*. 1517. In *Luther's Works*. American ed. Philadelphia: Fortress; St. Louis: Concordia, 1955–.

———. *Freedom of a Christian*. 1520. In *Luther's Works*. American ed. Philadelphia: Fortress; St. Louis: Concordia, 1955–.

———. *Heidelberg Disputation*. 1518. In *Luther's Works*. American ed. Philadelphia: Fortress; St. Louis: Concordia, 1955–.

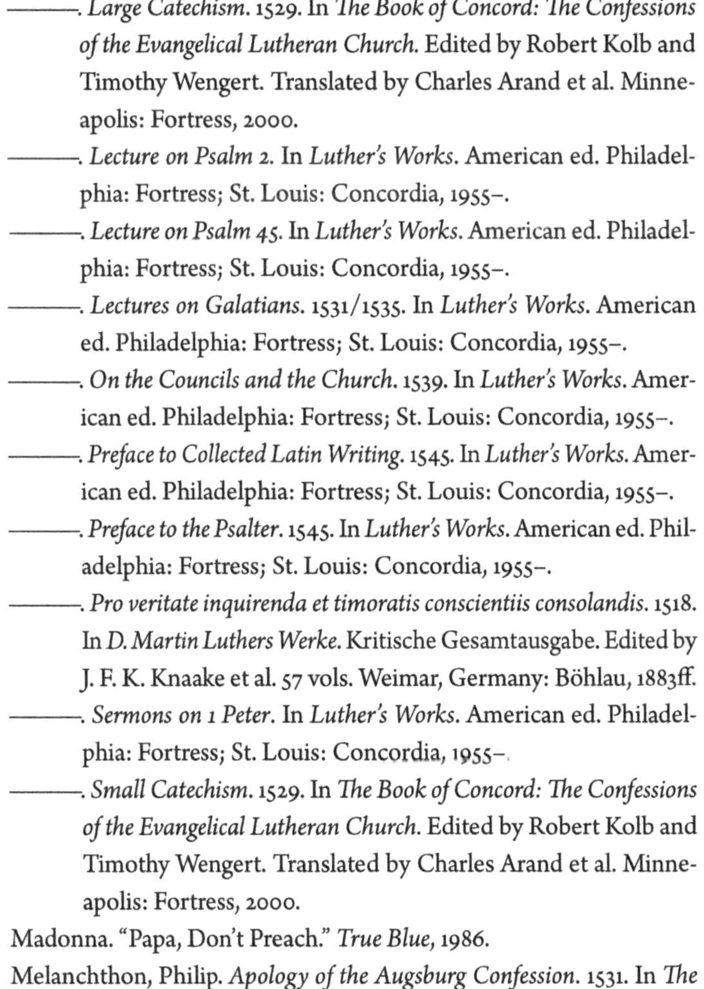

———. *Large Catechism*. 1529. In *The Book of Concord: The Confessions of the Evangelical Lutheran Church*. Edited by Robert Kolb and Timothy Wengert. Translated by Charles Arand et al. Minneapolis: Fortress, 2000.

———. *Lecture on Psalm 2*. In *Luther's Works*. American ed. Philadelphia: Fortress; St. Louis: Concordia, 1955–.

———. *Lecture on Psalm 45*. In *Luther's Works*. American ed. Philadelphia: Fortress; St. Louis: Concordia, 1955–.

———. *Lectures on Galatians*. 1531/1535. In *Luther's Works*. American ed. Philadelphia: Fortress; St. Louis: Concordia, 1955–.

———. *On the Councils and the Church*. 1539. In *Luther's Works*. American ed. Philadelphia: Fortress; St. Louis: Concordia, 1955–.

———. *Preface to Collected Latin Writing*. 1545. In *Luther's Works*. American ed. Philadelphia: Fortress; St. Louis: Concordia, 1955–.

———. *Preface to the Psalter*. 1545. In *Luther's Works*. American ed. Philadelphia: Fortress; St. Louis: Concordia, 1955–.

———. *Pro veritate inquirenda et timoratis conscientiis consolandis*. 1518. In *D. Martin Luthers Werke*. Kritische Gesamtausgabe. Edited by J. F. K. Knaake et al. 57 vols. Weimar, Germany: Böhlau, 1883ff.

———. *Sermons on 1 Peter*. In *Luther's Works*. American ed. Philadelphia: Fortress; St. Louis: Concordia, 1955–.

———. *Small Catechism*. 1529. In *The Book of Concord: The Confessions of the Evangelical Lutheran Church*. Edited by Robert Kolb and Timothy Wengert. Translated by Charles Arand et al. Minneapolis: Fortress, 2000.

Madonna. "Papa, Don't Preach." *True Blue*, 1986.

Melanchthon, Philip. *Apology of the Augsburg Confession*. 1531. In *The Book of Concord: The Confessions of the Evangelical Lutheran Church*. Edited by Robert Kolb and Timothy Wengert. Translated by Charles Arand et al. Minneapolis: Fortress, 2000.

Nickelsburg, G. W. E., and J. C. VanderKam. *1 Enoch: A New Translation*. Minneapolis: Augsburg Fortress, 2004.

Nietzsche, Friedrich. *Beyond Good and Evil: Prelude to a Philosophy of the Future*. Translated by Helen Zimmern. In *The Complete Works of Friedrich Nietzsche*. Edited by Oscar Levy. Vol. 5. Edinburgh: T. N. Foulis, 1909.

Ortega y Gasset, José. *The Revolt of the Masses*. 1929. Routledge Library Editions: Political Protest. New York: Routledge, 2021.

Percy, Walker. *Love in the Ruins*. New York: Picador, 1971.

Philo of Alexandria. *On Moses*. Translated by F. H. Colson. Loeb Classical Library 289. Cambridge, MA: Harvard University Press, 1935.

Pindar. "Pythian VIII." In *The Odes of Pindar Including the Principal Fragments with an Introduction and an English Translation by Sir John Sandys, Litt.D., FBA*. Cambridge, MA: Harvard University Press; London: Heinemann, 1937.

The Pretenders. "I'll Stand by You." *Last of the Independents*, 1994.

Ritter, Josh. "Girl in the War." *The Animal Years*, 2006.

Rowe, C. Kavin. *Christianity's Surprise: A Sure and Certain Hope*. Nashville: Abingdon, 2020.

Rutherford, Mark. *The Revolution in Tanner's Lane*. Edited by Reuben Shapcott. London: Trübner & Co., 1887.

Seneca. *On Benefits*. Translated by Miriam Griffin. In *The Complete Works of Lucius Annaeus Seneca*. Chicago: University of Chicago Press, 2014.

Senkbeil, Harold L. *The Care of Souls: Cultivating a Pastor's Heart*. Bellingham, WA: Lexham, 2019.

Shakespeare, William. *Macbeth*. Edited by Barbara A. Mowat and Paul Westerine. New York: Simon & Schuster, 1992.

Simon & Garfunkel. "Bridge over Troubled Water." *Bridge over Troubled Water*, 1970.

Sophocles. *Antigone*. In *The Three Theban Plays*. Translated by Robert Fagles. New York: Penguin Books, 1984.

Spufford, Francis. *Unapologetic: Why, Despite Everything, Christianity Can Still Make Surprising Emotional Sense*. London: Faber & Faber, 2012.

Tolkien, J. R. R. *The Return of the King: Being the Third Part of The Lord of the Rings.* Boston: Houghton Mifflin, 1993.

Virgil. *The Aeneid.* Translated by Robert Fagles. New York: Penguin Classics, 2006.

Webber, Andrew Lloyd. "Masquerade." *The Phantom of the Opera*, 1986.

Wenham, Gordon. *Exploring the Old Testament: A Guide to the Pentateuch.* Downers Grove, IL: InterVarsity Press, 2003.

Wesley, Charles. "And Can It Be, That I Should Gain?" In *The Hymnal 1982.* Church Pension Fund, 1982.

Wesley, John. *Journals and Diaries.* In *The Works of John Wesley.* Nashville: Abingdon, 1995.

Westerholm, Stephen. *Preface to the Study of Paul.* Grand Rapids: Eerdmans, 1997.

Wilder, Thornton. *Alcestiad.* In *Collected Plays and Writings on Theater.* Edited by J. D. McClatchy. New York: Library of America, 2007.

———. *The Angel That Troubled the Waters.* In *The Angel That Troubled the Waters and Other Plays.* New York: Coward McMann, 1928.

———. *The Woman of Andros.* New York: Longmans, Green, 1930.

"World Death Rate Holding Steady at 100 Percent." *Onion*, January 22, 1997.

Zahl, David. *Seculosity: How Career, Parenting, Technology, Food, Politics, and Romance Became Our New Religion and What to Do about It.* Minneapolis: Fortress, 2019.

Zahl, Paul F. M. *Peace in the Last Third of Life: A Handbook of Hope for Boomers.* Charlottesville, VA: Mockingbird Ministries, 2020.

Index of Subjects

Index of Scripture